AFRICAN-AMERICAN CIVIL WAR MEDALS OF HONOR

Randy Bishop

Author's Tranquility Press
MARIETTA, GEORIA

Copyright © 2021 by Randy Bishop

All rights reserved. No part of this publication may be reproduced, distributed or transmitted in any form or by any means, including photocopying, recording, or other electronic or mechanical methods, without the prior written permission of the publisher, except in the case of brief quotations embodied in critical reviews and certain other noncommercial uses permitted by copyright law. For permission requests, write to the publisher, addressed "Attention: Permissions Coordinator," at the address below.

Randy Bishop /Author's Tranquility Press
2706 Station Club Drive SW
Marietta, GA 30060
www.authorstranquilitypress.com

This is a work of non-fiction.

Ordering Information:
Quantity sales. Special discounts are available on quantity purchases by corporations, associations, and others. For details, contact the "Special Sales Department" at the address above.

African-American Civil War Medals of Honor/ Randy Bishop
Paperback: 978-1-7374522-7-0
eBook: 978-1-7374522-8-7

This book is dedicated to Harvey Warrner, my favorite Hoosier and a long-time Chicago Bears fan, for his friendship as well as his continued encouragement and support of my projects.

"I hope again to see you. I must bid you farewell should I be killed. Remember, if I die, I die in a good cause."

—Federal veteran of the American Civil War

Contents

INTRODUCTION 9
Aaron Anderson (aka Sanderson) (1811-1866) 14
Bruce Anderson (1845-1922) 18
William Barnes (1845-1866) 27
Powhatan Beaty (1837-1916) 33
Robert Blake (1834-?) 44
James Bronson (1838-1884) 50
William Brown (1836-1896) 56
Wilson Brown (1841-1900) 59
William Carney (1840-1908) 64
Clement Dees 72
Decatur Dorsey (1836-1891) 74
Christian Abraham Fleetwood (1840-1914) 80
James Gardiner (Gardner) (1839-1905) 93
James Harris (1828-1898) 99
Thomas Hawkins (1840-1870) 102
Alfred Hilton (1840-1864) 107
Milton Holland (1844-1910) 113
Miles James (1829-1871) 123
Alexander Kelly (1840-1907) 128
John Lawson (1937-1919) 133
James Mifflin (1839-?) 138
Joachim Pease 141
Robert Pinn (1843-1911) 146
Edward Ratcliff (1835-1915) 152
Andrew Jackson Smith (1843-1932) 159
Charles Veale (Veal) (1838-1872) 170
Endnotes 173

INTRODUCTION

Estimates hold that there were over 180,000 African Americans who served the United States Army during the War Between the States. Comprising the enlisted men in approximately 170 units, these men suffered from racist policies and mindsets of varied nature. An estimated 29,511 African Americans served in the Federal Navy.[1] Like their soldierly counterparts, these sailors were often victims of widespread animosity.

At the onset of the American Civil War, severe reluctance existed on the part of Federal officials regarding the enlistment of African Americans. An August 1861 First Confiscation Act proclaimed, "All enslaved persons fighting or working for the Confederate military were freed and relieved of obligations to their masters." The Militia Act of 1862, passed in July of that year, altered that mindset as it had become an "indispensable military necessity" to encourage black males to "help save the Union." With the implementation of the Emancipation Proclamation in January 1863, the War Department of the United States "authorized the recruitment of African American soldiers." General Ulysses Grant came to hold the opinion that the term "powerful ally" applied to African Americans.[2]

On May 22, 1863, General Order Number 143 created the Bureau of Colored Troops to "facilitate the recruitment of Black soldiers to fight for the Union

Army." The Bureau was soon renamed the United States Colored Troops and oversaw the aforementioned 170 regiments and almost 180,000 soldiers. The ability to join the cause of the Union had been predicted, as Frederick Douglass had said, "We are ready and would go." Douglass had also exclaimed, "Once let the black man get upon his person the brass letter, U.S., let him get an eagle on his button, and a musket on his shoulder and bullets in his pocket, there is no power on earth that can deny that he has earned the right to citizenship."[3]

It is likely most African American men who served the United States during the war held a mindset similar to that of a soldier who wrote to his family, "I hope again to see you. I must bid you farewell should I be killed. Remember, if I die, I die in a good cause." As Bob Farrell, a researcher of African American units recalled "It was their country, and they wanted to defend it. Their neighbors were enlisting and going to war; however, by law, that option was not available to them."[4]

African American soldiers quickly banished the stereotypes existing in relation their fighting abilities. Black infantrymen proved their bravery at Milliken's Bend, Louisiana; Port Hudson, Louisiana; Honey Springs, Indian Territory; Petersburg, Virginia; Fort Wagner, South Carolina; New Market Heights (Chaffin's Farm), Virginia; and Nashville, Tennessee. It was at the latter battle where one veteran noted, "The blood of the white and black man has flowed freely together for the great cause which is to give freedom, unity, manhood and peace to all men..." In the Campaigns that took place in the 1864-1865 period, African Americans took part in all except General Sherman's Georgia invasion.[5]

Disproportionate casualty and death tolls struck the ranks of African American units. For example, during the battle of New Market Heights, over 1,300 of the 3,000 black troops engaged were killed, wounded, or missing in just over an hour of combat. The African American soldiers comprised approximately twenty percent of the total Federal force in that engagement, yet their casualty figures accounted for a much larger percentage.[6]

Historian Jim Percoco penned, "On the day that Lee surrendered at Appomattox Court House, Virginia, on May 9, 1865, there were more African American soldiers fighting for the Union than the total of all Confederate forces. Interestingly, an estimated 2,000 black men, serving in one of seven units, were in the vicinity of Appomattox on that fateful day. Percoco also acknowledged that over 40,000 African Americans were killed in the course of the war.[7]

Additional information indicates that 30,000 African Americans, or 75% of the total deaths of black men in the Civil War, were from disease or infection. African Americans who voluntarily served the United States were in infantry and artillery units. They also assisted in noncombat functions such as carpenters, cooks, guards, scouts, teamsters, nurses, and chaplains.[8]

If captured, black soldiers were likely to "be returned to their previous owners, sold into slavery, or even hanged." As members of the United States military, blacks were often relegated to digging trenches, using inferior equipment, or suffering from "inadequate medical treatment in racially segregated hospitals."[9]

Among other difficulties African American soldiers faced during the early years of their enlistment was pay discrepancy. While White soldiers earned $13 per month, an African American infantryman received $10 per month. A $3 clothing allowance was also deducted from the pay African Americans were paid; no deduction was subtracted from White soldiers. It has been recorded that many African Americans protested this practice and refused any pay until the June 15, 1864 act that granted equal pay, equipment, arms, and healthcare for all soldiers, regardless of race. It has been written that "Lincoln...and Congress dragged their feet on this matter..."[10]

Despite these seemingly insurmountable odds, African American soldiers prevailed in the War Between the States. The late historian Brian Pohanka proposed, "Despite prejudice, unequal pay, and innumerable hardships, these brave black soldiers exemplified the idealism and sacrifice of men with a cause."[11]

The bravery of over twenty African American soldiers and sailors were duly recognized with the presentation of the Medal of Honor to those individuals. Over 1,000 Medals of Honor were earned in the American Civil War, the highest number of any United States conflict. The twenty-six African Americans who serve as the subjects of this manuscript were among those 1.000 Medal recipients of "the highest military honor an American soldier can receive, earned by actions that go above and beyond the call of duty."[12]

The first Medals of Honor that were designed and approved were for the Navy. The Congressional Medal of Honor Society explains, "The initial work was done by the Philadelphia Mint...The selected Medal of Honor design consisted of an inverted 5-pointed star. On each of the five points was a cluster of laurel leaves to represent victory, mixed with a cluster of oak to represent strength." The Medal of Honor Society added, "Surrounding the encircled insignia were 34 stars, equal to the number of stars in the U.S. Flag at the time."[13]

Two engraved images were inside the circle of thirty-four stars. Minerva, the Roman goddess of wisdom and war, was on the right side. As for the left side of the Medal, "Recoiling from Minerva is a man clutching snakes in his hands. He represented discord...Taken in context of the Civil War soldiers and sailor struggling to overcome the discord of the states and preserve the Union; the design was as fitting as it was symbolic."[14]

The original Medal's ribbon was "...a blue bar on top and 13 red and white stripes running vertically. The 13 represents the original 13 colonies...white represents purity and innocence, red represents hardiness, valor and blood, blue signifies vigilance, perseverance, and justice." Lastly, the rays of the sun were symbolized with the use of the white stripes.[15]

In the following chapters, this book will explore the lives and historic actions of the African Americans who earned the Medal of Honor for their services during the American Civil War. The time frames involved in the due recognition for these men, as well as the means by which they earned their Medal, vary greatly. However, as the words of each chapter will disclose, their struggles were common in that they fought for freedom of their race and to reunite their nation, The United States of America.

CHAPTER ONE

Aaron Anderson
(aka Sanderson) (1811-1866)

Although he became the first African American Medal of Honor recipient from the Navy, little is known about Aaron Anderson's life outside of the pinnacle of his military service. It is generally regarded that he was born on a farm near Plymouth, North Carolina in 1811. At some point in his life, he moved to Philadelphia, Pennsylvania and secured a job as a cook. Anderson remained in Philadelphia until the American Civil War reached its midpoint.[1]

On April 17, 1863, the fifty-two-year-old Anderson enlisted in the Navy in the city of his residence. Anderson was stationed aboard the *U.S.S. Wyandank* where he would be given the task of serving as an oarsman. There appear to be indications of an error at the point of his enlistment as Aaron Anderson's name was entered on the ship's log as Sanderson.[2]

Interestingly, the vessel on which Anderson served was also known to have another spelling to its name; *Wyandank* was also sometimes spelled *Wyandanck*. The *U.S.S. Wyandank* was a wooden-hulled ferry that was built in New York City in 1847. On September 12, 1861, the Navy purchased the *Wyandank* from the Union Ferry Company of Brooklyn. In turn, the one hundred thirty-two and a half foot *Wyandank* was assigned to duty as a stores ship in what was deemed the Potomac Flotilla.[3]

Aaron Anderson's boat, as well as other such vessels assigned to the Potomac Flotilla, owed its government service to James H. Ward. In 1861, Ward had asked Navy Secretary Gideon Wells to spearhead the formation of a group of ships to maintain the safety of the Chesapeake Bay area. Ward was shot through the stomach in June 1861, becoming the first United States Naval officer to be killed during the American Civil War. In the ensuing years, command of the flotilla eventually fell upon Commander Foxhall Parker.[4]

In March 1865, *U.S.S. Wyandank* ventured into Westmoreland County, Virginia and Mattox Creek. The creek was just short of fourteen miles in length, and it served as a tributary of the Potomac River. Rich in history, Mattox Creek is situated between the birthplaces of George Washington and James Monroe. Having grown into a significant trade port for items such as tobacco, the area had become an operations area, becoming a Confederate supply base, particularly on the right bank of the waterway. For that reason, Aaron Anderson joined his fellow crewmen as they approached the area.[5]

Wyandank, in conjunction with ships such as *U.S.S. Don* and *U.S.S. Stepping Stone* patrolled Mattox

Creek in order to block or destroy the Confederate supply line. On March 17, 1865, Anderson stayed aboard *U.S.S. Wyandank* while some seventy-foot soldiers patrolled the shore. Anderson and others on the *Wyandank* moved up Mattox Creek and witnessed three schooners that appeared to be abandoned.[6]

Ensign Summers operated the rudder of *Wyandank* while Boatswain Patrick Mullen guided a howitzer launch along the waterway. Two vessels approached the first of the three schooners. Anderson and others deemed as landsmen manned the oars of *Wyandank* when Confederate snipers opened fire on the ship. An estimated force of four hundred men in gray began shooting at the Federals, and the shots became so heavy that half of the oars were rendered inoperable. The barrel of a musket used to return fire against the Confederates was also cut in two. In addition, holes were punctured along the side of *Wyandank*.[7]

Aaron Anderson remained at his post and managed to guide the boat to safety, doing so while no serious injuries were inflicted upon the crew of *Wyandank*. T.H. Eastman commanded *U.S.S. Don* and wrote that "the crew aboard [*Wyandank*]...were all black but two." Eastman added that Anderson and a white boatswain's mate, Patrick Mullen, were "reported to me by Acting Ensign Summers as having assisted him gallantly."[8]

Anderson's Medal of Honor citation was awarded on June 22, 1865. Given the award with Mullen, Anderson received the recognition under the name Sanderson, as was entered on the ship's log. The wording of Anderson's citation stated in part, "Participating with a boat crew in the clearing of Mattox Creek...[Anderson]...carried out his duties courageously in the face of devastating fire..."[9]

Within a month of the time of Anderson's heroic actions at Mattox Creek, the Confederate surrender at Appomattox occurred. Anderson soon left the Navy. Sadly, little is known about his post-war life, a fact that again becomes muddied with the duality of his surname. Indications are that Aaron Sanderson returned to Philadelphia and worked in the southern part of the city for approximately twenty years. The Sanderson surname also appears as that of a widower residing at 1357 Kater Street in Philadelphia. Indications are that Anderson primarily engaged in vocations such as a laborer, coachman, cook, and whitewasher.[10]

Aaron Anderson, also known as Sanderson, suffered from heart disease, and passed away on January 9, 1886. He was buried at Philadelphia's Lebanon Cemetery.

CHAPTER TWO

Bruce Anderson
(1845-1922)

Bruce Anderson was born June 19, 1845. A number of sources record the location of his birth in Medico City; but others note the town of Mexico, located in Oswego County, New York, as the site of the event. However, the free-born Anderson was living in Gloversville, New York at the onset of the American Civil War, reportedly working on his family's farm.[1]

On August 12, 1864, young Bruce Anderson journeyed to Schenectady, New York, and he enlisted in Company K of the 142nd New York Volunteer Infantry. As such, he became one of few African-American soldiers to belong to a mixed-race military unit, from an enlisted man's perspective. While most African-Americans were only allowed to serve in companies of U.S. Colored Troops with other men of color, and they were subjected to doing so under the command of white officers, Anderson's enlistment in the 142nd New York was a rather uncommon situation. However,

Schenectady was located in St. Lawrence County, New York, a long-time stronghold of abolitionists and antislavery individuals. Interestingly, his Medal of Honor paperwork records his point of enlistment as Albany, New York rather than Schenectady.[2]

In December 1864 Anderson's corps was merged into a newly-formed 24th Corps. As such, Anderson was then in the First Brigade and the 2nd Division. On Christmas Day 1864, a little more than four months after enlisting, Private Bruce Anderson joined his comrades as they landed north of Fort Fisher, North Carolina.[3]

By late 1864, Wilmington, North Carolina, was the last significant Confederate port. The Federal blockade had become so effective, that items such as tobacco and cotton, usually exchanged for European goods, had few locations from which they could enter or exit the South. Fort Fisher's primary purpose was to defend or protect Wilmington. Proving the effectiveness of Fort Fisher to that time, blockade runners had been able to pass Union ships in the area and provide needed supplies to the Confederates in the area.[4]

Using the design of the Malakoff Tower in Ukraine, Fort Fisher was largely constructed from sand and dirt mounds, giving the installation the ability to absorb cannon projectiles more effectively than many of the brick-and-mortar forts of the era. In time, Fort Fisher was placed under the command of Colonel William Lamb. Colonel Lamb had received word from General Robert E. Lee that if Fort Fisher fell, there would be no chance to effectively supply Lee's Army of Northern Virginia.[5]

The men of the 142nd New York Volunteer Infantry were initially intended to participate on an assault against Fort Fisher. The onset of the engagement failed to produce the desired results for members of the Federal command, and the advance was suspended after the regiment endured total casualties of twenty killed and wounded. Company K joined the other companies of the 142nd as they vacated the area of Fort Fisher.[6]

Although the initial Federal attack had been repelled, it attained some success. A New York regiment involved in the advance had managed to capture some of the Confederate defenders and a battle flag. During the interrogations of the prisoners, it was determined that "the whole opposition of the Confederates was so weak that the officers believed the fort could have been taken with a small loss." Hearing reports of this intelligence, General Ulysses Grant became determined that a second attack should be made against the Confederate position at Fort Fisher.[7]

Within three weeks of the abandoned assault against Fort Fisher, a renewed effort was undertaken. By that time, Bruce Anderson's regiment was under the leadership of Colonel Newton Martin Curtis, and it would be among the first to attack the Confederate installation.[8]

During the second attack, the firepower inside Fort Fisher was formidable. Twenty-two guns placed on twelve-foot-high mounds faced the sea entry. Twenty-five cannon, atop massive hills that ranged from forty-five to sixty feet in height faced any land invasion on the fort's southern side. Bombproof shelters and subterranean corridors served the Confederate inhabitants.⁹

On January 12, 1865, Colonel William Lamb noted the extensive Federal fleet that approached Fort Fisher. Lamb recalled, "From the ramparts of Fort Fisher, I saw the great armada...the next morning revealed to us the most formidable armada the world had ever known, supplemented by transports carrying about 8,500 troops." Lamb's declaration was not inaccurate, for the ensuing action against Fort Fisher was the war's largest amphibious operation and contained an estimated sixty vessels.¹⁰

A sense of foreboding apparently reigned among the Confederate leaders inside Fort Fisher. Major General William Henry Chase Whiting had earlier begged for reinforcements from General Braxton Bragg; however, Bragg felt the troops were more strategically placed nearer Wilmington. When a small group of reinforcements reached Fort Fisher, Whiting stated to Lamb, "...my boy, I have come to share your fate. You and your garrison will be sacrificed."¹¹

Major General Alfred Terry was in charge of the Federal ground troops attacking Fort Fisher, while Rear Admiral David Porter led the approach from sea. Brigadier General Charles Paine was to attack the north side of Fort Fisher, while Brigadier General Adelbert Ames led his command against the strong sand and earthen sides.¹² Bruce Anderson was in the latter group.

Prior to the implementation of the Federal ground assaults, Porter's ships began a bombardment of Fort Fisher. Throughout the days of January 13 and 14, 1865, Federal shells struck Fort Fisher with such regularity that the Confederate inhabitants were unable to repair the damages inflicted upon the structure. In addition, the shots from Porter's ships rendered all but four of Fort Fisher's guns inoperable.[13]

Colonel Curtis and General Terry asked for some dozen volunteers to move ahead of the main Federal force and make an effort to charge over open ground in front of Fort Fisher. Armed only with axes, these volunteers were to attempt to create breaches in the massive pine fence that defended a portion of the Confederate earthworks. It has been noted that Private Anderson was not among the original group of volunteers, but he quickly asked to take the place of a fellow townsman who had volunteered. The gentleman from Gloversville, New York who Anderson desired to replace was a married man and a father of two children.[14]

Bruce Anderson and the 142nd New York joined three other regiments in the land approach against Fort Fisher. Their advance would target a massive palisade of wooden stakes where Confederate sharpshooters awaited any advancing enemy soldiers. Joining Anderson was Alaric Chapin, a seventeen-year-old from upstate New York. One of the men who also volunteered with Anderson was a Canajoharie, New York resident named Zachariah C. Neahr. Known as "Z.C." among his friends, Neahr knelt to pray before the other axmen volunteers and he made their way toward the Confederate stronghold. General Terry reportedly had tears in his eyes when he witnessed Neahr praying. Neahr told a friend after the battle that at the moment of his prayer, "…I gave up my life for my country."[15]

The group of volunteers, including Anderson, made their advance against fire from Confederate sharpshooters. Terms such as "withering" and "intense" were used to describe the gunshots the Confederates directed toward Anderson and his fellow ax-wielding Federals. Through extreme fortune, members of the volunteers, Anderson among them, managed to reach the log wall and cut a hole in it. After Anderson and his fellow volunteers chopped their way into Fort Fisher, they joined their armed comrades and fought through a mile and a half of Confederate defenses. Wilmington, North Carolina fell to the Federal forces the next month.[16]

Colonel Curtis was among the seventy-nine casualties the 142nd New York suffered during the assault against Fort Fisher. Initially thought to be mortally wounded, Curtis survived the serious injury and was later promoted to the rank of brigadier general. His actions at Fort Fisher also earned Curtis the designation of "Hero of Fort Fisher."[17]

Confederate General Whiting had earlier proclaimed that his fate was similar to that of the fort in that he would be sacrificed. When Whiting witnessed Federal troops entering the breach which Private Bruce Anderson and his fellow volunteers had created Whiting lead a counterattack against the men in gray. In the ensuing moments Whiting was given several opportunities to surrender, but he refused to comply. Confederates turned their guns toward Whiting who was severely wounded in his leg and captured. Whiting was taken to Fort Columbus, New York where he died of dysentery in the prison hospital March 10, 1865.

Ironically, decades later his body was moved to a cemetery in Wilmington, the very city he was trying to defend at the time of his capture.[18]

Although the small group of axmen had managed to cut a hole in the wall that allowed other soldiers to take the fort, the task was not accomplished without a significant loss. Most of the volunteers who had carried axes toward Fort Fisher had been killed in the early stages of the attack. The survivors included Anderson, Neahr, Alaric Chapin, George Merrill, and Dewitt Hotchkiss.[19]

Major General Adelbert Ames was so pleased and impressed with the performance of the group of volunteers that he recommended that the Medal of Honor be awarded to a total of thirteen men. By some stroke of misfortune, the letter Ames compiled for the reason of requesting the Medals was misplaced. It would be years before any of the thirteen men received due recognition. As a side-note, over fifty soldiers would eventually earn Medals of Honor for their exploits at the battle of Fort Fisher.[20]

In 1890 Zachariah Neahr petitioned for his Medal of Honor and received it on September 11 of that year. Neahr passed away from the effects of tuberculosis in 1903. Brigadier General Newton Martin Curtis was awarded the Medal of Honor on November 28, 1891, twenty-six years after the attack against Fort Fisher.[21] Still, Anderson and the remaining members of the volunteers who carried axes against the Confederate fort failed to gain their due recognition.

Anderson's post-war years involved him living in Illinois before returning to Amsterdam, New York. He also married twice and is recorded as having children from both marriages. His wife Julia James Anderson passed away in 1914.[22]

In 1914, Anderson hired a lawyer for the purpose of securing the receipt of a Medal of Honor. The intervention of the attorney resulted in the U.S. Army adjutant general opening an investigation into the lack of proper recognition for Private Anderson. In the process, the letter General Ames had penned decades earlier was discovered.[23]

On December 28, 1914, Private Bruce Anderson and two of his fellow survivors of the attack against Fort Fisher, were awarded the Medal of Honor. President Woodrow Wilson, celebrating his fifty-eighth birthday on the day of the ceremony, presented Anderson with the decoration. Anderson was acknowledged for "his own heroism" displayed during the assault. The text of Anderson's Medal citation partially proclaimed, "Voluntarily advanced with the head of the column and cut down the palisading." The prolonged process resulted in Anderson's Medal of Honor being one of the last given for service in the American Civil War.[24]

On the same day Anderson received his Medal of Honor, Alaric Chapin, by then a sixty-seven-year-old grandfather, and George Merrill, New Yorkers from Ogdensburg and Queensbury, respectively, were also awarded with the same. Sadly, Dewitt Hotchkiss, another individual who was listed on the long-lost letter from General Ames, was overlooked again and did not receive an award. Other men who helped to chop their way into the nine-foot wall at Fort Fisher were never honored. They included Jimmy Spring, Edward Petrie,

George Hoyt, Samuel Porteous, David Morgan, Silas Baker, Eugene Cooper and William McDuffie.[25]

Bruce Anderson died August 22, 1922 in St. Peter's Hospital of Albany, New York. His body was interred in Green Hill Cemetery Amsterdam. Like many of his fellow Medal of Honor recipients from the decisive action at For Fisher, Anderson's recognition was long overdue. Today his contributions, as well as those of his fellow volunteers, are commemorated at Fort Fisher State Historic Site.[26]

CHAPTER THREE

William Barnes
(1845-1866)

While the exact date is uncertain, 1845 is the typical year given for the birth of William Henry Barnes. A biographical sketch from the Maryland Archives differs in that respect, noting 1830 as the year Barnes was born. Additionally, one set of his enlistment papers state that he was twenty-three at the time of his 1864 enlistment, a statement that adds more confusion to the situation as either 1840 or 1841 would fit into that scenario. However, St. Mary's County, Maryland is the consensus location of the event of his entry into the world.[1] Aside from being a farmer, there is basically nothing else known about the pre-war years of Barnes.

William Henry Barnes joined Company C of the 38th United States Colored Infantry February 11, 1864. Serving as a private, Barnes was able to take part in the situation created for black troops when the United States Army created military units that were to be filled with men of color. Enlisting at a recruiting station at Point Lookout, Maryland, Barnes was recorded as being a thirty-three-year-old farmer. Again, his age and the exact date of his birth prove to be points of contention. Additional information on his record notes that his height was five feet eleven inches and had black eyes, black hair, and a black complexion.[2]

The 38th United States Colored Infantry Regiment was originally composed of free men and escaped slaves of the St. Mary's County, Maryland vicinity. Organized in Virginia January 23, 1864, the regiment consisted of Marylanders and Virginians, and it was in its infancy when Private William Henry Barnes joined its ranks.[3]

In the ensuing months, Barnes and his comrades saw action of varying degrees at locations such as Norfolk and Portsmouth, Virginia, where they were attached to the Departments of Virginia and North Carolina. In August 1864, the 38th United States Colored Troops were assigned to the 2nd Brigade, 3rd Division, 18th Corps of the Army of the James.[4] It was in that organization that Barnes was to gain his most notable service.

In the meantime, Confederate defenses around Richmond, Virginia, the capital city of the seceded Southern states, had been in the developmental stages since the early days of the war. As Federal attempts to take the Confederate capital had failed throughout the same period, Major General Benjamin Butler devised a plan to attach Richmond from a different direction. Using a line of attack that stretched from New Market Road southward to the James River, Butler felt an assault against the men in gray would prove successful.[5]

On September 29, 1864, Private Barnes and his fellow members of the 38th U.S. Colored Troops joined men from the 4th, 5th, 6th, and 36th U.S.C.T. in a division at Chaffin's Farm or New Market Heights. Located approximately eight miles southeast of Richmond, the area would serve as the initiation for the African American troops in respect to leading an assault. In addition, Major General Butler held the objective of capturing Richmond, an act that would boost morale among Northern soldiers and civilians who were largely disenchanted with the war's progress.[6]

Barnes joined the ranks of soldiers who were hungry, tired, and suffering from the losses of stragglers. Major General David Birney ordered the men of the United States Colored Troops to prepare for battle without benefit of ingesting hot food and with little time to rest. Although Generals Birney and Butler held to the belief that the Federal attack would come as a surprise to the Confederate defenders, the opposite was the situation. By 4 a.m. on September 29, Confederate soldiers were eating breakfast and preparing for the Federal advance.[7]

The initial Federal advance was to come from the members of the 4th and 6th United States Colored Troops. Defense of the Confederate position was the responsibility of five infantry regiments of Colonel Frederick Bass and Brigadier General John Gregg. Two distinct lines of gray-clad soldiers were established behind abatis that encumbered any sudden march into the Confederate works. In addition to these strong defensive qualities, several hundred yards of ground divided the Federal position from that of the Confederates.⁸

Musket discharges penetrated the darkness at 5:30 a.m., signaling the onset of the battle. Swamps delayed some of the Federal soldiers, while others traversed a rising plain some estimated five hundred yards in length. One historian wrote, "The Confederate defenders put down their coffee, picked up their rifles and...searched for their targets." A Federal officer stated that as his men approached the Confederate defenses, "...they entered the fog that enwrapped them like the mantle of death."⁹

Confederate fire from the defenses was described as "withering," and Texas troops under the command of Brigadier General John Gregg captured or inflicted casualties upon approximately half of the men in blue. In fact, the ferocity of Federal fire is proven from a brief view of Confederate casualties. An estimated eighty-seven percent of the men in the 6th U.S.C.T were killed, wounded, or captured at Chaffin's Farm. Forty-three percent of the Federal casualties in the battle were from members of the United States Colored Troops. This is even more tragic when taken with the fact that African American troops only comprised a small portion of men in blue at the location.¹⁰

Men of the 4th U.S.C.T. became entrapped in the line of chevaux-de-frise, a defensive technique that involved implanted logs containing drilled holes that held a series of crisscrossed sharpened wooden stakes. It was stated that the regiment was literally blown apart.¹¹

From a description in the Official Records, Private Barnes was said to have been "among the first to enter the works, although wounded..." One of the two men who joined Barnes in the early penetration of the Confederate defenses bayoneted and shot a Confederate officer. A Texas Confederate wrote, "I want to say...in my opinion, no troops up to that time had fought us with more bravery than did those Negroes."[12]

On April 6, 1865, Barnes was presented with the Medal of Honor for his actions at the Battle of Chaffin's Farm. Two other members of the regiment joined Barnes in the receipt of the Medal of Honor from their displays of heroism at Chaffin's Farm. Those men were James Harris, who also suffered multiple wounds, and Edward Ratcliff. Harris shared another common trait with Barnes in that both men were from St. Mary's County, Maryland.[13]

Subsequent action in which Barnes participated included the October 1864 battles of Deep Bottom and Fair Oaks. In November 1864, Barnes served in the trenches north of the James River. The following month the 38th U.S.C.T. was briefly attached to the 1st Brigade, 3rd Division, 25th Corps before being assigned to the 1st Brigade, 1st Division, 25th Corps by year's end. In the final months of the American Civil War, Barnes was primarily involved in the occupation of Richmond.[14]

Following the American Civil War, Barnes remained in the Army and reached the rank of sergeant on July 1, 1865, approximately three months after being awarded the Medal of Honor. Sergeant Barnes served briefly in frontier duty at Brownsville, Texas and at a number of locations along the Rio Grande and the Gulf Coast at Brazos Santiago, as well as Galveston. He eventually ended up in Indianola, Texas where he contracted tuberculosis.[15]

William Henry Barnes passed away December 24, 1866 in the Army hospital in Indianola, Texas. In doing so, he became one of one hundred ninety-two regimental members to die from disease in the unit's existence. Initially buried at Indianola, Barnes was later moved, along with other soldiers who had died in the area, and was reinterred in the San Antonio National Cemetery. Sadly, his remains lie in a common grave.[16]

The 38th United States Colored Infantry was mustered out of service weeks later, on January 25, 1867. The town of Indianola is a ghost town today, but a marker was placed in the San Antonio National Cemetery and serves as a memorial to Sergeant William Henry Barnes. His regiment is memorialized as well, with a statue in Lexington Park, Maryland serving as a tribute to all men who served in the United States Colored Troops.[17]

CHAPTER FOUR

Powhatan Beaty
(1837-1916)

Powhatan Beaty was born into the Richmond, Virginia slavery sector October 8, 1837. The names of his parents have apparently been lost to history. Little else is known about his early years or how and when he was able to leave the institution of slavery. However, Beaty, also spelled Beatty, ended up in Cincinnati, Ohio by 1849. There, Beaty gained an education, and he became interested in acting after his debut under the guidance of Professor Peter H. Clark. In addition to studying acting and elocution from Philadelphia-born stage actor James E. Murdock, Beaty also worked in a cabinet shop.[1]

The owner of the cabinet shop was Henry Boyd, a Kentucky-born slave who bought his own freedom at the age of 18. Under Boyd's direction, Beaty became highly efficient on the wood lathe. Beaty was one of Boyd's fifty employees, a group that consisted of black, white and immigrant workers who combined to produce the Boyd Bedstead. Because of his race, Boyd was unable to receive a patent for his bedsteads, but the popularity of the rounded side rails that screwed into the bedposts greatly increased the business's success.[2]

The 1860 Census recorded Powhatan Beaty as residing in the Henry Boyd home. Sadly, Boyd's successful factory was burned at the hands of angry whites. Quakers assisted in rebuilding the structure after the first two fires, but Boyd's inability to acquire insurance after an 1862 inferno led to the facility going out of business.[3]

Meanwhile widespread feelings of fear were commonplace among Cincinnati's Unionists in 1862, as rumors of a likely Confederate attack circulated among the city's residents. Confederates had been victorious at Richmond, Kentucky and had taken control of Frankfort, the capital of the Bluegrass State. Cincinnati, then the sixth largest U. S. city, held a large amount of Federal war material; most significant were the deposits of shoes, blankets, and overcoats. Should the Confederates capture or destroy those and similar items, the outcome could prove devastating to the Union war effort. Cincinnati's mayor, George Hatch, ordered all city businesses to close. Federal General Lew Wallace pronounced martial law for the city. That action also led to able-bodied African American men being forced from their homes as white soldiers used bayonets to drive the unwilling recruits toward a massive mule pen.[4]

A unit known as the Black Brigade, organized after General Wallace was informed of the treatment of the African Americans, was among the city's defense workers who were utilized to build fortifications around Cincinnati and dig tunnels beneath the Ohio River. Other duties of the Black Brigade included digging trenches and rifle pits, clearing area forests, and serving as the labor force for constructing roads in the vicinity of Cincinnati, the Queen City.[5]

Powhatan Beaty, in Company Number 1 of the 3rd Regiment, was among the members of the Black Brigade. Beaty participated in fifteen days of various construction details around Kentucky's Licking River. The first week was unpaid, but compensation increased to $1 per day for the second week. Another fifty cents per day was added for Beaty and his compatriots during the third week. Praising the efforts of these unwilling shovel handlers, General Wallace wrote, "...it will be said the spades and not the guns...saved the city from attack."[6]

William Martin Dickson, a Cincinnati judge, informed the members of the Black Brigade, "You have labored faithfully...The hills across yonder river will be a perpetual monument of your labors...Go to your homes with the consciousness of having performed your duty...bearing with you the gratitude and respect of all honorable men."[7]

Powhatan Beaty left the confines of Cincinnati in June 1863, and he joined the Federal Army in Camp Delaware, Ohio. Later renamed the 5th United States Colored Troops, Beaty's unit was initially designated as the 127th Ohio Volunteer Infantry. While at Camp Delaware, a recruiting station established exclusively for African-Americans, Beaty enlisted as a private. Beaty's period of enlistment was originally for three years, and two days into his military service, he was promoted to first sergeant. At the time, that rank was among the highest for men of color.[8]

First sergeant Powhatan Beaty was given the responsibility of overseeing forty-seven recruits and received orders to move to Columbus, Ohio. Early indications were that Beaty and those in his charge were to be subsequently sent to Boston where they would join Massachusetts units. However, information received in mid-June 1863 explained that regiments in Massachusetts were fully-manned and held no need for additional troops. John Mercer Langston requested permission to recruit an Ohio regiment of Colored troops, but his plea initially met objections. Ohio Governor David Tod countered Langston by saying, "To enlist a negro soldier would be to drive every white man out of the service." In time, Governor David Tod granted permission to form a regiment of African-Americans, and Beaty's contingent became the formative members of the 127th Ohio Volunteer Infantry on June 17.[9]

After being renamed the 5th United States Colored Troops, Beaty's group of Federal soldiers received approximately three months of training before moving toward Virginia.[10]

On September 29, 1864, Beaty and his comrades of the 5th United States Colored Troops joined other troops who were assigned to advance against the Confederate center at New Market Heights, Virginia. The location was also called, and regularly continues to be identified, by the alternative name of Chaffin's Farm.[11]

The strong Confederate defenses consisted of two formidable lines of abates reinforced with Confederate General John Gregg's Texas Brigade in a third line. The heavy Confederate artillery and musket fire resulted in horrendous casualties among the Federal attackers. Adding to the carnage was the fact Federal Major General Benjamin Butler had ordered the men of the Colored Troops to avoid firing their weapons until the Confederate position had fallen at the points of the Federal bayonets. Additional hardships and losses came from the natural elements of the presence of fog as well as swamps that fronted the Federal objective. The flag bearer of Beaty's Company G was one of many men in blue killed in the onslaught, and the ferocity of the battle soon led to a Federal retreat.[12]

During the confrontation, Sergeant Powhatan Beaty made his way through approximately 600 yards of withering gunfire in a return toward the Confederate stronghold. Beaty was able to retrieve the company flag and return it to the Federal line. Interestingly, Beaty not only carried out this heroic deed, but he also managed to be one of only sixteen enlisted men from a group of eighty-three to survive the action unwounded.[13]

Beaty, noticing none of the eight officers from Company G were not wounded, took command of the detachment. The ensuing second advance against the Confederate lines pushed the men in gray from their posts. The victorious assault resulted in three additional casualties for Company G. In turn, over fifty percent of the members of the division were wounded, captured, or killed. A modern historian has estimated that 1,027 black troops and white officers became casualties during the hour and a half combat at New Market Heights.[14]

The Confederate response to the heroism of Beaty and other African Americans in blue were varied, to say the least. One soldier in gray wrote, "...no troops to that time had fought with more bravery..." Another Confederate, a member of the same brigade countered, "Our men now have a perfect contempt for negro soldiers. It is almost a pity to put such things into battle."[15]

Powhatan Beaty's actions at New Market Heights received praises from General Benjamin Butler. The Federal officer promoted Milton Holland, one member of the 5th U. S. Colored Troops, to the rank of captain. However, the War Department reversed that due to the recipient's race. Butler explained his stance on the heroism of Beaty and his comrades by writing, "The colored soldiers...have silenced every cavil of the doubters of their soldierly capacity...Be it so, this war is ended when a musket is in the hands of every able-bodied negro who wishes to use one."[16]

General Butler used his own money to create and cast medals for one hundred ninety-seven veterans of the battle at New Market Heights. Known as the Butler Medal, the award was manufactured at the facilities of Tiffany & Company, and contained a red, white, and blue ribbon that hung from a silver base. At the end of the ribbon a wreath was engraved with "Army of the James." The face of the medals, issued due to what Butler deemed was a shortage of individuals being properly recognized, read, "Distinguished for Courage, Campaign Before Richmond, 1864." The back contained the words "US Colored Troops" and a Latin phrase that translated to "Freedom will be theirs by the sword."[17]

Additionally, on April 6, 1865, Beaty became one of fourteen African American soldiers to earn a Medal of Honor; the distinction was given for their conduct under fire during the battle of New Market Heights. The five-foot seven-inch tall Beaty's citation read that he, "...took command of his company, all the officers having been killed or wounded, and gallantly led it." One veteran of the engagement stated that the men each exhibited "unflinching heroism."[18]

The impact of the Federal victory at New Market Heights has been noted as providing a major stepping stone toward opening the door to Richmond, the Confederate capital. One historian exclaimed, "...where formidable earthworks were built to guard the New Market Road...the Northern plan succeeded. Relatively untested black soldiers...[advancing] against Southern veterans...dislodged that elite unit...from its defenses." Another added, "They had also wiped out effectually the imputation against the fighting qualities of the colored troops."[19]

Less than a month after the battle that resulted in Beaty's receipt of the Medal of Honor, he participated in the battle of Fair Oaks. Because of his actions in that engagement, Powhatan Beaty was mentioned in the Army of the Potomac's general orders. Colonel Giles Shurtleff, commander of the 5th Regiment, recommended promotions for Beaty on two separate occasions. While Beaty was given a brevet promotion to lieutenant, no positive actions were ever taken in regard to Shurtleff's suggestions. By the time of his discharge from the 5th Regiment, Powhatan Beaty had seen action in a large number of skirmishes and thirteen battles.[20]

Beaty returned to Cincinnati after the war, and on July 27, 1865, he married Mary Lee. The couple had several children, but only three, Albert Lee Beaty, Powhatan Beaty, and John Beaty, survived to adulthood. Albert Lee Beaty later served as an Ohio State Representative and was the Assistant U. S. District Attorney for Southern Ohio.[21]

In the subsequent postwar years, Beaty spent a short period of time as a porter aboard the Mississippi River steamboat *City of Vicksburg*. He later returned to Cincinnati where he worked as a janitor, began acting and worked in a cabinet shop. Other sources indicate that Beaty also served as a city engineer for the Cincinnati water works, but that paled in comparison to his acting abilities. By the end of the 1870s, Beaty's acting performances were gaining notoriety. Among those was a response Beaty provided during the 1878 celebration of Abraham Lincoln's sixty-ninth birthday. The

February 13, 1878 edition of *The Cincinnati Daily Star* noted that while a host of individuals toasted the memory of President Lincoln, "Mr. Powhatan Beaty responded in thrilling style 'The Oath,' by Thomas Buchanan Read." [22]

Aside from earning praises for his portrayal of characters such as Macbeth and Richard III, Beaty wrote an 1880 play entitled *Delmar, or Scenes in Southland*. The March 27, 1880 edition of *The Weekly Louisianan* recorded that Beaty "has high hopes of bringing it out... with a first-class colored troop and under a good manager." The play was never performed in public theaters, despite its popularity among privately-run venues. The following year he depicted the role of a plantation owner in *Delmar,* with the play set in the states of Kentucky, Mississippi, and Massachusetts. In 1884, Beaty joined forces with Henrietta Vinton Davis, a well-respected African-American actress, and spent much of the ensuing decade of the 1880s as her acting partner. Beaty and Davis organized a musical and dramatic festival in Melodeon Hall in Cincinnati. One review of Beaty's performance stated that he, "...threw himself into his part with masterly energy and power." Another proclaimed that Beaty, "wherever he has appeared, [is recognized] as a gentleman of the highest dramatic ability." [23]

During a D.C. amateur performance of scenes from *Macbeth, Richard III,* and *Ingomar,* more than 1,100 people, including famed abolitionist Frederick Douglas and his family, were in attendance. The May 7, 1884 production was reviewed in *The Washington Post,* and the reporter noted, "The earnestness and intelligence of several of the leading performers were such as to command the respect of those most disposed to find cause for laughter in everything that was said and done." A correspondent for The New York Globe stated, "...leap by leap the colored man and woman encroach upon the ground so long held sacred by their white brother and sister." Both articles addressed and condemned the conduct of many Caucasians who laughed and hurled insults toward many of the actors.[24]

Near the end of the decade, in 1888, Powhatan Beaty assumed the post of drama director of the Literary and Dramatic Club of Cincinnati, a group he also assisted in establishing. In addition, he devoted many of his remaining years to helping other African-Americans in Cincinnati to become more eloquent speakers. His time as an elocutionist also led to Beaty giving public readings for a variety of charities in the area.[25]

Beaty explained in an 1891 pension report that a skull fracture received from a fall during the charge at New Market Heights had contributed to his inability to effectively perform manual labor. As well, Beaty's failing eye sight added to the issue of his decreasing physical condition. Eight years later, Beaty lost his beloved wife, an incident that added to his burdens.[26]

Seventy-nine-year-old Powhatan Beaty died December 6, 1916. Insight into Beaty's later years, as well as praise for his character, appeared in an article from a Cincinnati paper. The obituary stated, "Powhatan Beaty, one of the old landmarks of Cincinnati...was for years in charge of the Thom's Building at Fifth and Main...and was known by every merchant and clerk in that district." The funeral for the Medal of Honor recipient was held at 628 West Seventh Street, "his late residence." He was buried in the Union Baptist Cemetery in Cincinnati. An Ohio Historical Marker was placed at the location of his burial in 2003.[27]

In 2001 two Virginia state legislators introduced legislation to name a bridge in honor of Powhatan Beaty. In turn, the Powhatan Beaty Bridge now allows passengers on Route I-895 to cross Virginia Route 5. Henry Marsh, who teamed with Dwight Jones to present the bill, proclaimed, "To recognize the heroism of Powhatan Beaty is the right thing to do. He was an extraordinary soldier and American. That's the kind of heroism that Americans have established over the years."[28]

CHAPTER FIVE

Robert Blake
(1834-?)

Robert Blake was reportedly born into slavery on a Virginia plantation. Another source states that a Charleston County, South Carolina plantation was the location of his birth. In addition to the uncertainty of his birthplace and date he entered the world, little is known about his early life. It appears that the Arthur Middleton Blake mansion, located on the Santee River farm where Robert Blake spent his years of servitude, was destroyed in an 1862 fire. The inferno that engulfed the plantation's main house, located approximately fifty miles north of Charleston, South Carolina, was the result of the Federal navy's venture along the waterway. The original intent of the Federal expedition was to destroy railroad bridges in the area. The Federals' first pass by the plantation had been peaceful, but during the return trip, the boats came under fire from the area of the Blake property.

Commander George Prentiss led a detachment ashore, and the Arthur Blake home and mill were burned, and over 100,000 bushels of rice were confiscated. With the destruction of the residence and the additional damage that was inflicted, approximately 400 slaves, including Robert Blake, left the area.[1]

The following year, Arthur Blake filed a claim of $288,375 in damages. The amount seems legitimate, as the 1860 Census reported the plantation owner held assets of $150,000 in real estate and $350,000 in personal property. Robert Blake's name was written on a list that included the names of 402 slaves for whom Arthur Blake sought compensation. The value placed upon Robert Blake was $1,100. Additionally, Robert Blake was noted as being 28 years old. That provides some indication as to his year of birth.[2]

The Arthur Middleton Blake property was reportedly "a Confederate regimental headquarters used to protect ships running the blockade on the South Santee." That indication, along with Arthur Blake's move to England at the onset of the Civil War, led to the denial of his claim for damages.[3]

Robert Blake and his recently displaced comrades boarded Federal naval vessels as contraband. The men were transferred to North Island, near Winyah Bay, a location situated in the vicinity of Georgetown, South Carolina. The camp quickly grew to a population of some 2,000 escaped slaves. In order to avoid a Confederate raid, the U. S. Navy relocated the camp to Hilton Head in March 1863. Near that time, Blake was made aware of a request for twenty single males to enlist for service aboard the *U.S.S. Vermont*. However, there is some question as to when and at what position Robert Blake enlisted in the Navy.[4]

Approximately one year later, *Robert* Blake had transferred to a gunboat, *U.S.S. Marblehead*. That ship, launched October 16, 1861, was described as "a two-masted schooner with rifled cannon." Descriptions of the ship also note that *Marblehead* had armaments of two 24-pound howitzers, a 20-pound Parrot rifle, and one 11-inch Dahlgren smoothbore.[5]

In June 1862, *Marblehead* was reassigned from the North Atlantic Blockading Squadron to the South Atlantic Blockading Squadron. Blake and his fellow crewmen aboard the *Marblehead* were under the leadership of Lieutenant Commander Richard Meade, the son of a naval officer and the nephew of Federal General George Meade. Blake served as a steward on the *Marblehead*. Blake was on the boat as it traveled along the Stono River and approached the town of Legareville on December 25, 1863.[6]

That Christmas Day would be far different from any other that Blake or the other 114 officers and crew aboard *Marblehead* had ever experienced. Legend holds that early on the morning of Christmas 1863, Confederate howitzer shells were launched toward the 158-foot boat as it approached John's Island. Lieutenant Meade reportedly left his bunk and arrived on deck in his night clothes. Blake, carrying the commanding officer's uniform, followed Meade, who subsequently struggled to change clothes in the midst of an attack. An exploding artillery round knocked down Blake as he stood on the gun deck. Sadly, the exploding shell also killed one of the gun's powder boys. It was recorded that

Robert Blake sprang into action and ran to the ship's magazine in order to retrieve powder for the ship's guns.[7]

Robert Blake approached one of the guns and manned it as *Marblehead* returned fire toward John's Island. The intensity and accuracy of the Federal fire from Blake's gun and others on his gunboat eventually caused the Confederates to abandon their post, despite twenty shells striking *Marblehead*. The Confederates not only left their position, but they also neglected to move a caisson and one of the guns used in the artillery attack. At least one account of the engagement reports that two 8-inch seacoast howitzers, rather than one, were apprehended. Blake, who had voluntarily left his non-combat role and assumed personal risk, was awarded the Medal of Honor.[8]

Lieutenant Commander Meade reported to Rear Admiral John Dahlgren and made mention of the actions of several sailors on *Marblehead*. Four of the men aboard the vessel would come to receive the nation's highest honor. In addition to Robert Blake, those sailors included Landsman Charles Moore, Boatswain's Mate William Farley, and Quartermaster James Miller. A noteworthy aspect of this battle and the rewarding of the medals is the varied background of the four recipients. Two were immigrants, one from Ireland and another Norway, one young man was from Maine, and Blake was an escaped slave. Regarding Robert Blake, Meade noted, "Robert Blake, a contraband, excited my admiration by the cool and brave manner in which he served the rifle gun." Meade went on to add, "I have again to commend the good conduct of everyone on board. Their courage was so well displayed that the enemy, who had doubtless counted on disabling us, were forced to retire...in confusion and ignominy."⁹

Robert Blake's Medal of Honor citation states, "On board the U.S. Steam Gunboat *Marblehead*, off Legareville, Stono River, December 25, 1863, in an engagement with the enemy on John's Island." The brief description of Blake's actions states, "Serving the rifle gun, Blake, an escaped slave, carried out his duties bravely throughout the engagement, which resulted in the enemy's abandonment of positions, leaving a caisson and one gun behind."¹⁰

Interestingly, Blake's rank was the only of the four recipients from the action to not be acknowledged. He was simply identified as "contraband." All four of the men were issued their awards with General Order 32. Their citations were dated April 16, 1864, approximately four months after the incident that resulted in their honors. Robert Blake also holds the distinction of being the first African American to win the Medal of Honor. It has been noted that while a medal was awarded to Sergeant William Carney for his July 1863 actions, Carney did not receive his award until 1900. Blake obtained his medal in 1864. Therefore, Carney was the African American who earned a Medal of Honor at the earliest date, but Robert Blake was the first to actually receive one.¹¹

After his receipt of the Medal of Honor, Blake reenlisted in the U. S. Navy as a seaman. Other than the fact Robert Blake was able to serve on the *U. S. S. Vermont* during his second term, nothing else is recorded in relation to his life.¹²

In 2013 the South Carolina Department of Motor Vehicles, under the suggestion of Senator John Scott, renamed its Orangeburg, South Carolina office in memory of Robert Blake. In doing so, DMV Executive Director Kevin Shwedo exclaimed, "We've got the opportunity to go ahead and recognize a real hero." Shwedo added that the designation of "hero" is readily used today, but recognizing Robert Blake and other Medal of Honor recipients in DMV offices across the state clearly honors men who bled for their nation.[13]

The town of Legareville, located near the site of Robert Blake's heroic actions, no longer exists. Many of the area families would often leave the region in the summer months, and they returned in fall, when the threat of malaria was minimalized. The war had brought about lengthy periods of abandonment, and the town fell victim to Union soldiers who plundered various structures. On August 21, 1864, an area resident took it upon himself to rid the Federals of additional possibilities for raids. The man wrote, "...I burnt Legareville." Sixteen other men set their own homes on fire. With that, the future of Legareville was lost.[14]

CHAPTER SIX

James Bronson
(1838-1884)

James H. Bronson was born in either Indiana County, Pennsylvania, or Trumbull County, Ohio; sources vary as to the exact location. The event presumably took place in the year 1838. Bronson moved from Indiana County at some point prior to the onset of the American Civil War, as the 1860 Census recorded Bronson as being a resident of Weathersfield Township in Trumbull County, Ohio.[1]

Twenty-five-year-old James Bronson left his vocation as a barber and enlisted for military service July 4, 1863 in Trumball County, Ohio, but one source proclaims that took place in Indiana County, Pennsylvania. Some six weeks later, on August 21, 1863, the five-foot nine-inch-tall Bronson was mustered into service at Camp Delaware, Ohio. Initially enlisting at the rank of private, Bronson was eventually promoted to first sergeant of Company D, 5th Regiment, United States

Colored Troops. That regiment later became known as the 127th Ohio Colored Volunteer Infantry.[2]

Just over a month after his enlistment, First Sergeant James Bronson took part in the September 29, 1864 battle of Chapin's Farm, an engagement also known as New Market Heights. The Virginia Foundation for the Humanities has noted that fourteen African-Americans eventually earned Medals of Honor for their actions during this battle. Interesting, that is all but one of the total number of medals awarded to United States Colored Troops during the American Civil War. That number does not reflect upon African American sailors who received the award.[3]

James Bronson took part in the Federal advance against the Confederate left where troops from Brigadier General John Gregg's Texas Brigade stood. Two strong lines of defense and intense Confederate fire greeted Bronson and his comrades. As will be reinforced through the related statements of those near him, James Bronson took command of Company D, rallied his fellow soldiers, and led another charge against the Confederate post. This was done after all of the company officers had been killed or wounded in the earlier attack. In respect to the intensity of the battle in which African Americans "fell by the scores," black soldiers who attempted to fire or load their weapons were "cut...down in huge numbers." Nonetheless, the Federal troops were able to capture Fort Harrison, their objective of the assault. One source recorded those eighty-five Federal enlisted men were killed and 248 wounded of the 550 engaged in the battle.[4]

Robert Pinn, a fellow soldier of Bronson's, noted the leadership skills Bronson exhibited from the onset of the battle. Pinn proclaimed that Bronson was, "...far more of the time in command of his company under the rank of First Sergeant."[5]

Accolades for James Bronson and his comrades were issued in the days after the action at Chapin's Farm. An October 11, 1864 dispatch from the Headquarters of the Dept. of Virginia and North Carolina declared, "In the charge on the enemy's works...at...New Market, better men were never better led...With hardly an exception officers of colored troops have justified the care with which they have been selected." Additional praise for members of the U.S.C.T. included, "A few more such gallant charges and to command-colored troops will be the post of honor in the American armies."[6]

Comments directly dedicated toward Bronson came from Major General Benjamin Butler who wrote, "This war is ended when a musket [is] in the hands of every able-bodied negro who wishes to use one...James H. Bronson, first sergeant...left in command, all...company officers being killed or wounded, and led them gallantly and meritoriously through the day."[7]

Bronson's actions were not completed without personal injury. Bronson recalled, "I was struck on the calf of left leg...lame for a few days. I have really large bunch of veins on [my] left leg and pain around my heart." Bronson added that years after the battle, "...if I exert myself to any extent my suffering about my heart and left side are so that I fall to the ground."[8]

Perhaps the greatest compliment to James Bronson's heroic actions from the battle of Chapin's Farm, Virginia is found in the citation that acknowledged

Bronson earning the Medal of Honor. That text stated, "The President of the United States of America, in the name of Congress, take pleasure in presenting the Medal of Honor to First Sergeant James H. Bronson, United States Army, for extraordinary heroism on 29 September 1864, while serving with Company D, 5th Colored Infantry...Bronson took command of his company, all the officers having been killed or wounded, and gallantly led it."[9]

The Medal of Honor was issued to James H. Bronson on April 6, 1865. Bronson also received the Butler Medal, an award that General Benjamin Butler designed and personally paid for in order to recognize the service and heroism of several African American veterans of the battle at Chapin's Farm.[10] In the meantime, changes in Bronson's rank and placement of service would take place. Additionally, not all of these alterations created positive outcomes for Bronson.

On November 30, 1864, James Bronson requested to be placed into membership in the Regimental Band. The contents of records related to that incident reflect that Bronson also asked for a reduction in rank. In turn, he was allowed to serve as a musician in the military brass band.[11]

Bronson's tenure as a member of the Regiment's Band came to an end when he was mustered out of service September 20, 1865. The musician reportedly concluded the military phase of his life at Carolina City, North Carolina. Interestingly, other indications are that Bronson's point of being mustered out was Columbus, Ohio.[12]

James Bronson spent the majority of his post-war years as a resident of Salem, Ohio and, later, Mansfield Valley, Pennsylvania. The 1870 Census indicated that he lived in Columbiana, Ohio with his wife, Ellen Bronson. The Bronson couple lived in an area that consisted of nine homes with one family in each structure. Records note that the area residents were 12 white males, 12 white females, 8 black females, and 7 black males. Bronson also served in the ministry from October 1873 until July 1881.[13]

Severe suffering from his leg wound continued to hamper Bronson. He tried to attempt to gain relief from an area doctor, but the doctor soon took exception to Bronson's political views. Bronson stated, "We differed as to who I should vote for. I wishing to vote for Major McKinley. My...family physician wishing me to support and work for Peter A. Laubie, which I refused to do, and he for that reason has refused to give me the desired affidavit and no other reason existing to the least of my knowledge and belief."[14]

Bronson's interaction with the physician continued when Bronson filed a complaint with the Pension Board in 1882. The issues related to this complaint and Bronson's inability to gain medical support for his claim were evidently never resolved.[15]

James Bronson passed away November 16, 1884, aged 45 or 46. He was buried in the Chartiers Cemetery in the Allegheny County Pennsylvania town of Carnegie. Bronson's grave came be found in the U.S. Veterans Section, Soldiers Tier 1.[16]

In 2014, a plaque honoring James H. Bronson was placed in the Hall of Valor at the Soldiers and Sailors

Memorial Hall and Museum in Pittsburgh, Pennsylvania. This particular honor is reserved for veterans with ties to the Keystone State and for individuals who were honorably discharged.[17] Thus, the accolades for James H. Bronson continue, more than a century and a half after his actions that earned him the Medal of Honor.

CHAPTER SEVEN

William Brown
(1836-1896)

William H. Brown was born in Baltimore, Maryland in 1836. Aside from the year, there is no information regarding a more specific date. Sadly, few facts are known about his pre-war life and activities. Aside from his birth, the next detail related to Brown is his enlistment date of March 23, 1864. At that time, William H. Brown was assigned the post of a landsman aboard the *U.S.S. Brooklyn*, a vessel that served in the West Coast Blockading Squadron of Rear Admiral David Farragut's fleet.[1]

The *U.S.S. Brooklyn*, launched in 1858, had served in the Caribbean in the years before the war. Since the onset of hostilities, the ship had taken part in the Federal blockade of the South and had seen action on the Gulf and Atlantic Coasts as well as the Mississippi River. The vessel was equipped with a ten-inch gun and twenty-nine-inch guns that had and would prove highly destructive to the Confederates.[2]

The crew of the *Brooklyn* entered Mobile Bay August 5, 1864. Intense fire from four Confederate ships and guns inside Forts Gaines and Morgan pelted *Brooklyn* and seventeen other Federal vessels of Farragut's squadron. At the time, Brown's primary duty centered upon his use of the shell whip, a mechanism that held the purpose of lifting boxes of gunpowder upward from below decks to the gun deck.[3]

As Brown's ship continued to take hits from the Confederate shells, Brown managed to keep moving ample amounts of gunpowder to the Federal guns. The primary opponent of the *Brooklyn* was the Confederate ironclad ram *C.S.S. Tennessee*. The vessel was a 1273-ton ram attempted to ram the *Brooklyn*, but the effort was fruitless. In a few short minutes, the *Tennessee* was the lone Confederate ship, and the ensuing hour-long battle yielded few positive results for the crew aboard the Confederate ironclad.[4]

When the action came to a conclusion, Brown and his cohorts secured the surrender of all Confederate ships in the vicinity. Federal land forces also managed to capture the defending Confederate land-based defenders. Accolades of the highest degree awaited the men aboard the *Brooklyn*. Despite fifty-four of its crew being killed and another forty-three wounded, the *Brooklyn* had fired one hundred eighty-three projectiles at the Confederates. Twenty-three sailors and marines on the vessel earned the Medal of Honor for their heroism displayed against the men in gray.[5]

On December 31, 1864, approximately four months after his acts of heroism, William H. Brown received the Medal of Honor. His citation stated, "On board the *U.S.S. Brooklyn* during the successful attacks against Fort Morgan rebel gunboats and the ram *Tennessee* in Mobile Bay on 5 August 1864. Stationed in the immediate vicinity of the shell whips which were twice cleared of men by bursting shells, Brown remained steadfast at his post and performed his duties in the powder division throughout the furious action which resulted in the surrender of the prize rebel ram *Tennessee* and in the damaging and destruction of batteries at Fort Morgan."[6]

William H. Brown died November 5, 1896 in Washington, D.C. The uncertainty of his birth date leads his age being either 59 or 60 at the time he passed. Brown was buried in Arlington National Cemetery. His grave is located in Section 27, Site 565-A of the Arlington, Virginia grounds.[7]

CHAPTER EIGHT

Wilson Brown
(1841-1900)

Wilson Brown was born in Natchez, Mississippi in 1841. Unfortunately, the month and day of his birth are not known. The names of his parents have also been lost to time. In fact, aside from James Surget's Carthage Plantation being the location of his birth, there is little information regarding his life prior to his enlistment in the United States Navy.[1] The circumstances surrounding the beginning of his tenure in the military were somewhat unique.

Wilson Brown was a slave near Natchez and witnessed the *U.S.S. Hartford* patrolling the Mississippi River in March 1863. Seizing the opportunity, Tom Gates, also a slave, and "Brown jumped into the treacherous waters and swam to one of the ships...The Union officers were so impressed with Brown's courage...they sent him to naval training..."[2]

Another source states that an additional reason for Brown enlisting in the navy was due to the fact that African Americans tended to be treated better in the navy than in other branches of the military. The pay was also reportedly greater in the navy. As such, Brown officially enlisted March 18, 1863. He was described as "a Contraband Negro" who was five feet, eight inches in height, and his age was noted as twenty-two.[3]

Upon his enlistment, Wilson Brown was given the assignment of landsman aboard the *U.S.S. Hartford*. The *Hartford* served as the flagship in Rear Admiral David Farragut's West Gulf Blockading Squadron.[4]

Holding the lowest rank in the navy, landsman Wilson Brown typically "performed menial and unskilled work" while on the *Hartford*. A usual assignment of Brown's was to serve as a shell-boy. As such, he had to maintain the cannon shells, keeping them clean and cutting the fuses to a length the gunner prescribed.[5]

On August 5, 1864, under the leadership of Rear Admiral Farragut, Wilson Brown and his fellow crewmen of the *Hartford* took part in the Battle of Mobile Bay. The fourteen wooden ships and four monitors of Farragut's fleet entered the bay at 6 a.m. The West Gulf Blockading Squadron was to participate in the completion of Operation Anaconda, Winfield Scott's plan to squeeze the life from the seceding states. Brown joined other sailors who worked on the berth deck of the vessel. Their tasks typically involved operating the shell whip, a mechanism that enabled boxes of gunpowder to be lifted onto the gun deck.[6]

Admiral Farragut's squadron began to receive fire from Confederate ships as well as guns of Forts Morgan and Gaines. The *U.S.S. Hartford* subsequently began returning fire toward the *C.S.S. Tennessee.* One Confederate shell exploded among Wilson Brown and five sailors as the group manned the shell whip. Brown was the fortunate member of the group, as he was the only one not injured or killed when the shell exploded.[7]

However, the explosion of the shell blew Wilson Brown into the hatch. Brown landed on the floor of the next lower deck and was knocked senseless. When Brown awoke, he had to pull himself from below the body of a dead crewmember. Returning to the shell whip, Wilson Brown discovered another African American, John Lawson, the only other survivor of the six men had also made his way to their post.[8]

Although John Lawson had been wounded in the leg, he refused medical attention. Wilson Brown joined Lawson as the two men managed to continue supplying gunpowder to the ship's guns throughout the remainder of the battle. The heroism of the duo resulted in them earning the Medal of Honor.[9]

The citation reflecting Wilson Brown's actions and explained the rationale behind him receiving the Medal of Honor stated, "On board the flagship *U.S.S. Hartford* during successful attacks against Fort Morgan, rebel gunboats, and the ram *Tennessee* in Mobile Bay on 5 August 1864. Knocked unconscious into the hold of the ship when an enemy shell burst fatally wounded a man on the ladder above him, Brown, upon regaining consciousness, promptly returned to the shell whip on the berth deck and zealously continued to perform his duties through four of six men at his station being killed or wounded by the enemy's terrific fire."[10]

On December 31, 1864, Wilson Brown was designated as a Medal of Honor recipient, one of twelve sailors aboard the *Hartford* so honored. The Home of Heroes proclaims that ninety sailors and eight marines received Medals of Honor for their parts in the battle at Mobile. That is the most for any single day in American history. As for Brown, he remained in the United States Navy until disability led to his discharge the following year.[11]

Wilson Brown made his postwar home in Natchez. There, he met and married Lizzie Walker. The couple never had children of their own, but they helped raise three children. One of the youngsters, future minister Benjamin Smith, was considered their godchild. The other two individuals who benefited from the benevolence of the Browns were Cynthia Brown Lewis and Bud Brown.[12]

Clermont Baptist Church, located on Cemetery Road in Natchez, also benefitted from Wilson Brown's work ethic. Brown was one of the founders of the congregation, and he served as a deacon. In 1881 Wilson and Lizzie Brown bought an acre of land on Cemetery Road where they built a small store and a house.[13]

Wilson Brown died January 24, 1900. Due to the uncertainty of his birthdate, Wilson Brown's age at the time of death was either 58 or 59. He was buried in the Natchez National Cemetery in the town of his birth. Of the more than 8,000 veterans interred at the location, Wilson Brown is the only Medal of Honor recipient.

Wilson Brown also holds the distinction of being the only Mississippian to win the Medal of Honor.[14]

Sadly, although Wilson Brown had named as a recipient of the Medal of Honor four short months after battle in which he earned it, he never personally received the award. In 1956, over half a century after his death, Brown was finally recognized as a Medal of Honor recipient. Additional delays negated the family of Wilson Brown being presented the long overdue recognition until 1982.[15]

CHAPTER NINE

William Carney
(1840-1908)

William Harvey Carney was born into slavery in Norfolk, Virginia February 29, 1840. At least one source notes that William Carney's father, also known by the name William, used the Underground Railroad as a means to escape slavery. After William Sr. earned sufficient funds to purchase the freedom of his wife and son, the reunited family made their way to New Bedford, Massachusetts. The Carneys' new city of residence was a whaling port that also held a "vibrant African American community."[1]

The Carney family evidently held a high admiration for education. Before the group had moved to Massachusetts, they managed to break the societal norm of the times and secured William, Jr. a spot in a private school in Norfolk, Virginia. William Harvey Carney managed to not only learn to read and write, but he also excelled in his quest to become a superb student.[2]

Indications are that young William Harvey Carney was also a religious individual who had dreams of entering the ministry. However, the overwhelming situation that presented itself soon after President Abraham Lincoln issued the Emancipation Proclamation caused William Jr., like many of his peers, to alter his plans and join the Federal forces. Lincoln's document, effective in early 1863, authorized the recruitment of African Americans into the military.[3]

William Carney described his changing concept of his religious calling in an article from an 1863 issue of *The Liberator*. Carney stated, "I had a strong inclination to prepare myself for the ministry, but when the country called for all persons, I could best serve my God serving my country and my oppressed brothers."[4]

Within a few weeks, William Carney joined a locally-raised militia, the Morgan Guards, a group that eventually became Company C of the 54th Massachusetts Colored Infantry Regiment. The 54th Massachusetts was reportedly the first Federal black unit. Leadership of the 54th Massachusetts rested upon a white officer in his mid-twenties, Colonel Robert Gould Shaw, the son of wealthy Boston abolitionists.[5] The 54th, as well as other units of African American composition, were prohibited from having black men holding an officer's rank.

William Harvey Carney's educational background and the leadership skills soon resulted in his promotion to the rank of sergeant. One author stated that because of Carney's "education, brilliance, and potential strength in leading others," he was quickly placed into the position.[6]

William Harvey Carney's first exposure to combat occurred at James Island, South Carolina. Although the 54th Massachusetts had gone two days without sleep and had little access to rations, Colonel Robert Gould Shaw volunteered the regiment, previously assigned to menial tasks, to lead the assault against Fort Wagner. The fort was a heavily-fortified Confederate installation, also known as Battery Wagner, and it served as one of the points of defense for Charleston. If that position were to fall to Federal troops, the city and its harbor would be closer to becoming a Confederate loss.[7]

Fort Wagner had been named for Lieutenant Colonel Thomas M. Wagner, a South Carolinian. The Confederate installation measured 250 by 100 yards, and it contained fourteen cannons. Any attempted approach toward the 1,700-man fort had to cross a ten-foot wide and five-foot deep ditch containing water. Land mines and palmetto stakes provided additional obstacles for attacking forces.[8]

The 54th Massachusetts was initially situated on a sand dune approximately 1,000 yards from Fort Wagner. Land and sea artillery had shelled the Confederate fort most of the day, presumably enabling the nighttime approach to be made more successfully. As the sun set, the 54th Massachusetts prepared to attack in two wings that each consisted of five companies.[9]

Captain Luis Emilio, a member of Company F in the 54th Massachusetts, recalled the situation his comrades and he faced as they were approximately 200 yards from Fort Wagner. Emilio noted, "Wagner became a mound of fire, from which poured a stream of shot and shell...A sheet of flame, followed by a running fire...swept along the parapet."[10]

Colonel Shaw, surrounded by men of his 600-member command, became pinned down at the base of Fort Wagner's parapet. Shaw attempted to rally his men and inspire them to continue their advancement against the fort.[11] The intensity of the battle increased, and tragedy lay in store for many of those who had enlisted in the 54th Massachusetts.

John Wall carried the national flag as the group had moved toward Fort Wagner. A report in the *New York Herald* stated that Wall "...fell into a deep ditch, and called upon his guard to help him out...but Sergeant William H. Carney, of Company G, caught the colors." Seeing the color bearer fall, Carney grabbed the colors, preventing them from hitting the ground. Carney then made his way up the parapet in an effort to inspire his compatriots to follow his example.[12]

William Harvey Carney told a slightly altered account and recalled that he found the banner in the sand, threw away his gun, "seized the colors and made my way to the head of the column." Flashes from the Confederate weapons lit up the darkened sky and revealed the devastation their guns had inflicted upon the men of the 54th Massachusetts. Carney held the flag as Colonel Shaw once again attempted to rally his troops.[13]

Colonel Robert Gould Shaw stepped upon the rampart of Fort Wagner. Captain Emilio recalled, "He stood there for a moment with uplifted sword, shouting, 'Forward, Fifty-fourth!' and then fell dead, shot through the heart, besides other wounds." Private Thomas Burgess was near Colonel Shaw when the officer was killed. Burgess received a serious wound near the same moment Shaw was struck. Burgess reinforced much of Emilio's version of Shaw's tragic death.[14]

Sergeant William Harvey Carney also climbed atop Fort Wagner's rampart and hoisted the U.S. flag at the Confederate stronghold. Carney remarked, "All around me were the dead and wounded, lying one upon the other." Feeling a sense of Godly intervention, Carney said, "It seemed a miracle that I should have been spared in that awful slaughter." Carney stated that the scenes of blood caused him to enter a brief state of stupor...when he came to his senses, he found himself alone at the top of the embankment. Carney noted, "It were folly for me to try to advance, so I dropped to my knees around my dead comrades, and I laid as low and quiet as possible."[15]

Carney recalled that musket balls and canister rounds were spraying sand into the air, and he "was almost blinded" as the dirt flew around him. Confusion seized the moment as Sergeant Carney struggled to determine his surroundings. He recalled, "I could see dimly on one side a line of men mounting the ramparts and going down into the fort. I thought they must be our own men, but in the light of cannon flash I saw they were the enemy."[16]

Reaching the conclusion that the Federal advance against Fort Wagner had failed, William Carney wrapped the flag around the staff and began his retreat from the installation. He jumped into a rifle pit situated near the outer perimeter and hit a wooden support. Carney's fall bruised his breastbone, but a more significant injury lay ahead. Within seconds of falling, William Carney received a bullet wound to his left hip. The projectile fractured his thighbone; Carney fell again.[17]

An article from *The New York Herald* said of Carney, "He brought the colors off, creeping on his knees, pressing his wound with one hand and with the other holding up the emblem of freedom." A New York soldier offered assistance to Carney who refused to yield his flag to anyone who was not in the 54th Massachusetts. A canister shot then struck Carney's head, but he managed to keep the flag from striking the ground. Carney eventually located a corpsman who was able to direct him to approximately two dozen men and an officer from the 54th Massachusetts. The battle may have likely proven more devastating for the 54th Massachusetts had reinforcements not arrived and enabled the bullet-ridden survivors to withdraw.[18]

The officer who provided assistance to Carney was Lieutenant Alexander Johnston of Company F. Carney presented the flag to Johnston as members of the

54th Massachusetts cheered Carney. Carney proudly stated, "Boys, the old flag never touched the ground."[19]

The casualties for the 54th Massachusetts during the engagement at Fort Wagner were tremendous. The regiment suffered 272 killed, wounded, or missing from the 600 men who engaged in the battle. Confederate casualties were listed as totaling 174.[20]

The wounded Sergeant Carney was sent to a military hospital and was unable to return to the 54th Massachusetts for five months. Carney's wounds proved severe enough that he was discharged from Federal service in June 1864. William Carney then returned to New Bedford, served as the superintendent of streetlights, and married Susanna Williams October 11, 1865.[21]

William and Susanna Carney moved to California in the late 1860s. William Carney worked for a real estate company before the couple returned to New Bedford, Massachusetts in 1869. Carney then took a job as a letter carrier, and he regularly told his story about his exploits at Fort Wagner. He was noted as saying, "I only did my duty." Carney was also a founding member of the Robert G. Shaw Post of the Grand Army of the Republic in New Bedford.[22]

William Carney's bravery at Fort Wagner would not go unnoticed. On May 9, 1900, he was awarded the Medal of Honor for his actions during the July 1863 battle of Fort Wagner. The significance of this is stated in the words, "Owing to the fact that Carney's actions and achievements preceded those of other Medal honorees, historians consider him as the first African American to be bestowed the Medal of Honor."

However, Robert Blake holds the distinction of being the first African American to receive the award. Carney's date of heroism is earlier than that of any other recipient, making his date of merit for the award somewhat of a milestone.[23]

William Harvey Carney's Medal of Honor citation read, "When the color sergeant was shot down, this soldier grasped the flag, led the way to the parapet, and planted the colors thereon. When the troops fell back, he brought off the flag, under fierce fire..."[24]

After serving as a letter carrier for thirty-two years, Carney retired from the United States Post Office in 1901; he then took a job as a messenger at the State House in Boston. A tragic accident involving an elevator mangled Carney's leg that had been so viciously injured at Fort Wagner. The effects of the wounds sustained from the elevator proved too strong for Carney. William Harvey Carney passed away on December 9, 1908 at the age of sixty-eight, leaving his wife and a daughter, Clara.[25]

The flag atop the Massachusetts Capitol was flown at half-staff in his memory. Never before had such an honor been paid to a citizen who was not an official. The man regularly regarded as the first African American Medal of Honor recipient was buried in Oak Grove Cemetery in New Bedford, Massachusetts. Carney's Suffolk County plot is located in Section LL, Lot 78.[26]

CHAPTER TEN

Clement Dees
(Unknown birth and death dates)

A unique situation involves the Medal of Honor recipient Clement Dees. Little information exists about Dees aside from the events related to his award. Those facts are few, but significant nonetheless.

Clement Dees was born in Cape Verde, near the West Coast of Africa. At some point he arrived in the United States and eventually ended up as a seaman aboard the *U.S.S. Pontoosuc*. That vessel, a 1173-ton *Sassacus* class double-ender steam gunboat, had been built in Portland, Maine.[1]

During the military engagements on the Cape Fear River of North Carolina, Clement Dees and seven of his shipmates were noted for their actions that led to the capture of Fort Fisher and Wilmington. The battles took place between December 4, 1864 and February 22, 1865. On March 31, 1865 Commander William Temple wrote the Secretary of the Navy and recommended the men as recipients of the Medal of Honor.[2]

Clement Dees deserted his ship in Boston, Massachusetts on February 18, 1865 as the Navy was demobilizing it. The Medal of Honor that was intended to belong to Dees was then revoked.[3] No additional information related to the life or career of Clement Dees is available.

CHAPTER ELEVEN

Decatur Dorsey
(1836-1891)

Decatur Dorsey was born a slave in 1836 at New London, Maryland. The plantation on which he was born and raised belonged to a wealthy land owner whose property possessions were described as "extensive." The Howard County, Maryland town was located near New Market. Interestingly, Dorsey's birth occurred before Howard County was known by that name; it was called the Howard District of Anne Arundel County at the time of his coming into this world. Little information exists in relation to his younger years. There is a family proclamation that a brother of Decatur Dorsey started a New London church that exists to this day. Additionally, no known photograph of Decatur Dorsey has been positively identified.[1]

The National Park Service has documented that Decatur Dorsey's owner released him in March 1864. Other accounts declare Dorsey escaped from slavery near that time. An enlistment bounty was paid to Edward

Rider, Jr. for Decatur Dorsey, listed as Rider's slave. Regardless, on March 22, 1864 Dorsey enlisted in Company B of the 39th United States Colored Infantry, U.S.C.T., in Baltimore, Maryland. His enlistment stated that Dorsey was a laborer at the time he joined the military, adding debate to the events surrounding his time of leaving slavery. Dorsey evidently managed to impress those around him, for he was promoted to corporal May 17, 1864.[2]

During his initial weeks as a member of the 39th Regiment, U.S.C.T., Decatur Dorsey took part in the campaign from the Rapidan to the James River in Virginia. That occupied time during May and June, 1864. The unit also guarded trains of the Army of Potomac during the Wilderness and Petersburg Campaigns.[3] A major change lay ahead for the recognition and prestige of the regiment.

Decatur Dorsey and the 39th U.S.C.T. soon made their way to Petersburg, Virginia. There, a standoff between the Confederate and Federal forces had resulted in the opposing lines reaching a close proximity of only 400 feet, particularly near the Confederate position known as Elliot's Salient. The men in blue became determined to dig a tunnel under the Confederate lines and detonate an estimated four tons of explosives to annihilate the rebel soldiers in that vicinity.[4]

In an attempt to bring the existing siege to an end, the Federals detonated explosives just before 5 a.m. on July 30, 1864. The resulting blast created a 200-foot gap in the Confederate lines. Federal troops made a determined effort to use the hole to enter the

Confederate works. Sadly, the assaulting Federals ran into the crater, rather than around it, soon creating a killing field for the defending Confederates. Many men in blue who ventured into the crater found themselves in a death trap as Confederates fired into the attacking Federal ranks.[5]

Ordered to provide relief and rescue to those trapped in the area of the recently-created abyss, Decatur Dorsey's regiment left their reserve position and participated in the Battle of the Crater at Petersburg on that fateful date of July 30, 1864. Some reports indicate that the original Federal battle plan was to use the African American troops to lead the charge, but General George Meade apparently altered his strategy in the hours before the event. Meanwhile, Dorsey carried the regimental flag as his compatriots charged through the crater and moved toward the Confederate line. It was regarded that the color bearers were extremely courageous in battle because of the situations in which they regularly found themselves. Color bearers, because of their significance to the organizational aspects of their regiments, were often the targets of enemy sharpshooters. Due to the fact they often lacked the possession of a weapon during battle, they also had limited abilities to defend themselves. It is noteworthy to point out that the dangers of a common color bearer would have likely been increased when an African American carried the regimental colors of a Federal unit while fighting on a Southern battlefield.[6]

The men of the 39th U.S.C.T. were able to break into the Confederate defenses, but a counterattack pushed back the men in blue. Decatur Dorsey used his determination and waved the flag; in doing so, he rallied his fellow soldiers for another attack. Intense hand-to-hand combat ensued, with Dorsey and the men of the 39th U.S.C.T. capturing approximately two hundred Confederates and two flags. The intensity of the battle eventually overwhelmed the Federal warriors, and they were forced to retreat from the Confederate stronghold.[7]

One description of Dorsey's actions of the day stated, "He saw a field...covered with...blood and bodies. He charged...ahead of 1,000 men, planted his flag on the hill..." An additional quote proclaimed, "Decatur Dorsey saved the reputation of the Union Army...in war, one thing counts: courage."[8]

While the actions of Decatur Dorsey and other Federal soldiers who took part in the action at the crater were full of heroism, mixed reviews of their conduct were also readily stated. Newspapers across the nation, as well as some of their Caucasian compatriots blamed the African American troops for the heavy casualties and ultimate defeat that befell the Federal forces at the crater. Some 5,300 men were wounded or killed in the general time frame.[9]

Decatur Dorsey's Medal of Honor citation was issued November 8, 1865. It said, "The President of the United States of America, in the name of Congress, takes pleasure in presenting the Medal of Honor to Sergeant Decatur Dorsey, United States Army, for extraordinary heroism on 30 July 1864, while serving with Company B, 39th U.S. Colored Infantry, in action at Petersburg, Virginia. Sergeant Dorsey planted his colors on the Confederate works in advance of his regiment, and when the regiment was driven back to the Union works, he carried the colors there and bravely rallied the men."[10]

In the months after the action at Petersburg, the 39th U.S.C.T. took part in battles such as Weldon Railroad, Poplar Grove Church, Boydton Plank Road, and Hatcher's Run. Fort Fisher, Wilmington, Raleigh, and Bennett's House were also additional actions of the regiment.[11]

Evidence indicates that Dorsey was promoted to the rank of sergeant two days after the engagement at the Crater. He became First Sergeant Dorsey, the highest noncommissioned rank during the war, in June 1865. On December 4, 1865, while in Wilmington, North Carolina, he received an honorable discharge. The Medal of Honor recipient married soon after.[12]

Having moved with his wife, Mary Christy Dorsey, to Hoboken, New Jersey, from New York City, Dorsey apparently lived a relatively simple life as a laborer and sailor for the next two and a half decades. The effects of typhoid, rumored to have been contracted during a visit to Wilmington, and rheumatism, contributed to the death of Decatur Dorsey in 1891. The fifty-five-year-old Medal of Honor recipient was buried in an unmarked grave at Flower Hill cemetery in North Bergen, New Jersey. His grave was discovered and moved in 1984. Dorsey was reinterred in another location of the cemetery during a ceremony that included full military honors.[13] Decatur Dorsey's widow filed for a pension and received it in 1898. Unfortunately, the Medal of Honor that was awarded to Dorsey was lost after his death. According to his great-great-nephew, Lester Dorsey, that may have been due to

Decatur Dorsey having no children to whom the medal would have been bequeathed. On a positive note, a historical marker for Decatur Dorsey is located in Ellicott City, Maryland and conducts an overview of the man's life and his contributions.

CHAPTER TWELVE

Christian Abraham Fleetwood (1840-1914)

Christian Fleetwood was born July 12, 1840 in Baltimore, Maryland. His parents, Charles and Anna Marie Fleetwood, were free black residents of that city. Charles served as a majordomo, or head butler, for John Brune, a rich sugar merchant and chairman of Baltimore's chamber of commerce.[1]

Christian Fleetwood's level of education was extraordinary. His early endeavors into learning were under the guidance of John Brune. Evidence indicates that Brune and his wife, who resided in Baltimore's Mount Vernon District, with no children of their own, held Christian Fleetwood in high esteem and thought of Fleetwood as a son. Their extensive library was opened to young Fleetwood, and he immersed himself in the volumes it held.[2]

Fleetwood's additional studies, particularly in business, took place with Dr. James Hall, director of the Maryland Colonization Society, an organization that promoted free African Americans moving to Sierra Leone and Liberia. He visited those two nations when he was sixteen, and one Fleetwood historian has stated that the young man seriously considered leaving the U. S. for a life in Liberia. John Brune had sent Christian Fleetwood on a tour of the nation as training for the likelihood of the young man becoming the chief West African representative for Brune's sugar business. Despite the temptation to stay in Liberia and enjoy the well-paying opportunity the future held, Fleetwood determined that he would have a more significant impact upon the welfare of those held in bondage if he returned to the United States and worked for abolition. Fleetwood graduated as valedictorian from Oxford, Pennsylvania's Ashmun Institute, an all-black school that eventually became Lincoln University, in 1860.[3]

The 1860 Census listed Christian Fleetwood as a nineteen-year-old mulatto. His father Charles was noted as being a forty-four-year-old mulatto waiter; no occupation was displayed for his forty-four-year-old mulatto mother. Mrs. Fleetwood was listed as being illiterate. Another family member, Christian Fleetwood's twenty-year-old sister Averick, was also counted in the entries. Interestingly, Charles Fleetwood claimed owning $100 in personal property.[4]

Working some three years as a Baltimore shipping clerk and commission agent for G. W. S. Hall and Company, Fleetwood conducted business with Liberia and English entities. While in that vocation, he joined a group of Baltimore men and founded the *Lyceum Observer*, the first African American newspaper published in Maryland. The publication served as "a forum for the advancement of black rights." A deeply religious member of the Episcopal church, Fleetwood made frequent contributions to newspapers of that denomination. Among the periodicals for which he wrote was *Christian Recorder*. His religious convictions resulted in Fleetwood contemplating entering the ministry, but he eventually decided to forego that avenue.[5]

As the American Civil War progressed, Christian Fleetwood became compelled to offer his services to the U. S. military. Joining the 4th Regiment United States Colored Infantry on August 11, 1863, Fleetwood benefitted from his high level of education and was quickly promoted to sergeant major, the highest rank a black soldier could attain at that time. The promotion occurred August 19, 1863.[6]

Fleetwood and his 1,000 fellow members of the 4th United States Colored Infantry Regiment marched through Baltimore on September 17, 1863. The group left Camp Belcher, located on the western side of the city, and marched to the harbor. Sergeant Major Christian Fleetwood was in the front rank as the regiment proceeded through town.[7]

Throughout his time in the army, Fleetwood kept a diary that has been praised as clearly exhibiting "the rich texture of camp life and army routine." Many of his letters have also been preserved and are noted as "clear and concise...much more alive than many might expect."[8]

Responsible for much of the paperwork of his regiment, Sergeant Major Fleetwood made one diary entry that stated, "Reports in office. Oh Lord...the details." Another expressed, "Commenced discipline book." Typical Sunday entries centered upon his church activities and included one that said, "Prepared for church and attended. Good sermon." One historian clarified that Fleetwood's entries were usually short due to space constraints.[9]

The 4th U. S. C. T. was briefly stationed at Point Lookout, a prisoner-of-war camp that came to have a rather notorious reputation among its Confederate captives. Serving as the senior noncommissioned officer of the regiment, Sergeant Major Fleetwood had to create work details and duty rosters for the camp. This tandem responsibility was enlarged with his added assignment to keep order among the soldiers in his regiment. Fortunately, Fleetwood and the other members of the 4th U. S. C. T. were stationed at Point Lookout less than three weeks.[10]

Fleetwood's June 21, 1864 entry was noteworthy. In it, he wrote, "Division moved toward Pburg. Stopped in woods. Slept like a Dormouse. Woke and snacked. President Lincoln and Gen. Grant passed our bivouac and were cheered."[11]

Sergeant Major Christian Fleetwood's early tenure in the military has been recorded as "largely uneventful." Rarely did he see combat, but he was present at unsuccessful sieges of Richmond. However, the Federal forces had been pushed back twice when Fleetwood's regiment was still moving toward Richmond. While he could see some of the fighting at Petersburg, Fleetwood stood with his regiment in reserve throughout that action.[12]

While uninjured during the fighting at Chaffin's Farm, or New Market Heights as it is also known, Christian Fleetwood narrowly escaped harm as bullets tore into his clothing without striking him. This is a remarkable feat as his regiment recorded a casualty rate of fifty percent during the engagement. One historian specified that Fleetwood's trousers bore a bullet hole, his hair was singed, and the hearing in his left ear was greatly reduced. Fleetwood himself credited his ability to survive the battle to the fact he was a "little fellow," and the bullets passed above his head, although one cut his bootleg, trousers, and stocking.[13]

Fleetwood's account of the engagement at Chaffin's Farm was straightforward and read, "Line formed. Moved out & we charged with the 6th at daylight and got used up. Saved colors. Remnants of the two gathered and maneuvering under Col. Ames of the 6th U.S.C.T...." One historian offered that Fleetwood's two words, "Saved colors," described "...the single most memorable activity or event of his life."[14]

The actions of Christian Fleetwood during the September 29, 1864 engagement at Chaffin's Farm are certainly noteworthy. As the 4th USCT engaged the Confederates that day, Fleetwood saw the first regimental flag bearer fall. When the second did the same, Fleetwood moved toward the colors, grabbed the staff, and carried them throughout the remainder of the battle. Sergeant Major Fleetwood recalled that he managed to carry the flag during "a deadly hailstorm of bullets, sweeping men down as hailstones sweep the leaves from trees."[15]

Fleetwood recalled that the 4th U.S.C.T. lined up for their initial charge at New Market Heights with eleven officers and 350 enlisted men. He supervised the left side of the regiment. The ferocity of the battle in which the group took part is noted in Fleetwood's words, "When the charge was started our color-guard was complete. Only one of the twelve came off that field on his own feet. Most of the others are there still."[16]

Sergeant Major Fleetwood added, "Early in the rush one of the sergeants went down, a bullet cutting his flag staff in two and passing through his body." The bloodshed, as noted above, continued. Fleetwood explained, "The other sergeant, Alfred B. Hilton, of Company H, a magnificent specimen of manhood, over six feet tall and splendidly proportioned, caught up the other flag and pressed forward with them both."[17]

Speaking of Sergeant Hilton, Fleetwood lamented, "It was not long before he also went down, shot through the leg. As he fell, he held up the flags and shouted, 'Boys, save the colors.'" Fleetwood proclaimed that he grabbed the American flag, a gift from the "patriotic women of our home in Baltimore," and Corporal Charles Veal took the blue flag.[18]

The 125-pound Fleetwood noted that two lines of abatis and one of palisades protected the strong Confederate earthworks, making it "evident there was too much work cut out" for the assaulting Federals. Although Fleetwood and Veal managed to struggle through the first two lines and a few troops entered the palisades, Fleetwood felt the situation "was sheer madness, and those of us who were able I had to get out as best we could."[19]

Ensuing battles in which Sergeant Major Fleetwood took part included the assault against Fort Fisher, near Wilmington, North Carolina. A subsequent move inland involved Fleetwood and the 4th U. S. C. T. taking part in Major General William Sherman's operations that targeted Confederates under the command of Joseph Johnston.[20]

On April 6, 1865, six months after the battle of Chaffin's Farm, Sergeant Major Christian Fleetwood was awarded the Medal of Honor. He was one of fourteen African American soldiers to earn the honor for actions at New Market Heights/Chaffin's Farm. His citation read, "The President of the United States of America, in the name of Congress, takes pleasure in presenting the Medal of Honor to Sergeant Major Christian A. Fleetwood." Noting the specifics of Fleetwood's heroism, the citation noted that he, "...seized the colors, after 2 color bearers had been shot down, and bore them nobly through the fight."[21]

Another notable accolade for Sergeant Major Fleetwood lies in the fact that every officer surviving officer of the 4th Regiment U. S. Colored Infantry wrote to Secretary of War Edwin Stanton, asking for Fleetwood to receive an officer's commission. Based upon the racial segregation and policy in the period's military, Stanton did not grant the requests. However, Fleetwood did receive the Butler Medal, an award that Federal General Benjamin Butler created and financed for the men he felt had exhibited high courage and heroism.[22]

Although Fleetwood had once considered making a career in the military, a June 8, 1865 letter to his one-time employer, Dr. James Hall, indicated his dissatisfaction with the way in which the U. S. Army was treating black soldiers. Fleetwood penned, "Upon all our record there is not a single blot, and yet no member of this regiment is considered deserving of a commission or if so cannot receive one...I see no good that will result to our people by continuing to serve...A double purpose induced me and most others to enlist, to assist in abolishing slavery and to save the country...I think that a camp life would be decidedly an injury to our people."[23]

Suffering from an "intermittent fever," Christian Fleetwood spent a portion of October 1865 in an Alexandria, Virginia hospital. Quinine was among the medicines he received. Apparently becoming aware of the poor chances of surviving the confines of the medical facility in which he was a patient, Fleetwood left without permission and rejoined his regiment.[24]

Sergeant Major Christian Fleetwood was honorably discharged from the military May 4, 1866, the same day the 4th United States Colored Infantry

Regiment was mustered out of service. Indications are that he worked as a bookkeeper in a Columbus, Ohio grocery firm until 1867. Fleetwood married a Pennsylvania-born teacher named Sarah Iredell after the war and held various jobs, in and outside the Federal government, in Washington, D. C.[25]

In D. C., Fleetwood held vocations such as working in the Supreme Court building, the Freedmen's Bureau, and with the government of the District of Columbia. He also held a job with a realty company. A ten-year term as a bookkeeper in the D. C. brank of the Freedmen's Savings and Trust Company occupied most of the 1870's decade. In 1881, Fleetwood took a job as a clerk at the War Department; he held that post until his death.[26]

Continuing to serve his country, Christian Fleetwood organized a battalion of National Guardsmen for the D. C. area. Fleetwood was the group's commander, holding the rank of major. The unit was consolidated with others in 1891 and became the First Separate Battalion. When he was passed over as the leader of that group, Fleetwood resigned. He had also established the Colored High School Cadet Corps of the District of Columbia in 1888. That organization sought to establish a "high standard of military service for African American soldiers."[27]

In 1895, Christian Fleetwood published a pamphlet entitled *The Negro as a Soldier*. The manuscript was introduced at the Cotton Exposition in Atlanta. In the document, Fleetwood proclaimed, "...it is impossible only to indicate in skeleton the worth of the Negro as a soldier. If this brief sketch should awaken even a few to interest in his achievements, and one be found willing and fitted to write the history that is their due, that writer shall achieve immortality."[28]

Numerous citizens of D. C. requested that Christian Fleetwood be appointed to a command position of the 50th U. S. Colored Volunteer Infantry during the Spanish American War. The War Department disregarded the pleas, and the D. C. area soldiers' participation in the conflict was also put aside. Fleetwood's height of five feet four and a half inches, a factor he felt prevented serious injury at Chaffin's Farm, has been theorized as a major reason why he was not appointed to a commanding role in the Spanish American War.[29]

Fleetwood was known to have possessed a strong love of music. Four D.C.-area churches profited from Fleetwood's musical talents as he served as the choirmaster for each at various times. The congregations where he directed fellow musicians were St. Luke's and St. Mary's Protestant Episcopal Churches, Berean Baptist Church, and the 15th Street Presbyterian Church. Area newspapers frequently contained articles focused on choirs and groups Fleetwood led.[30]

On January 11, 1889, Christian Fleetwood was recognized in a proclamation bearing over one hundred signatures and addressed to, "The brave soldier and generous citizen." Published in the February 2, 1889 issue of *The Washington Bee,* under the article title of "Fleetwood's Testimonial," the proclamation stated in part, "The undersigned, your friends, acquaintances, and fellow citizens, desire...to give convincing and acceptable proof of their esteem for you...We recognize your patriotic services to the Union during the late Civil War, and since your muster out of services...your work among your fellow citizens for charity, benevolence, the church, and whatever has been for the good of the community."[31]

The article from *The Washington Bee* continued praising Fleetwood by saying, "You have never been called upon to give your services but that a ready response was forthcoming... much is due to your earnest and arduous labor, patient and painstaking interest." Summarizing the goals of the correspondence, a writer said, "We therefore, desire to tender you a testimonial in some substantial manner, so that you may better know how much you, your long and faithful services to your country and mankind...are appreciated."[32]

Six days after the Testimonial, Fleetwood responded, "I need not say...that the movement set forth...filled me with surprise not second to the gratitude and warm appreciation it has arouse in my being. For the past twenty-one years during which my lot has been cast with the people of this district, I have felt that their interest and mine were identical."[33]

Ever humble, Christian Fleetwood continued, "It was my duty to lend my efforts...to any good cause that needed assistance...I greet this offer as testifying that I perhaps have not altogether failed in my earnest efforts. I am honestly proud to the honored gentlemen whose names grace this highly prized letter, representing as they do every station in life and every denomination in religion."[34]

Fleetwood ended his statement of gratitude by inviting those honoring him to attend "one of the finest musical entertainments that has ever been offered in Washington…Again thanking you…with a depth to which language cannot give expression."[35]

A 1900 document listed Fleetwood's D. C. home as located on Spruce Street, where Christian and Sara Fleetwood, along with their sixteen-year-old daughter, Edith, resided. The Fleetwood family reportedly led an active social life in which his musical presentations and literary gatherings were favorably received. Among his supporters were Lucy Webb Hayes and Francis Folsom Cleveland, the wives of Presidents from the era. The home was razed in the 1990s. A historical marker is located at 319 U Street, NW; the former site of the home is a location on the African American Heritage Trail in D. C.[36]

Sara Fleetwood was a member of the first graduating class at the Freedmen's Hospital nursing school. Receiving her degree in 1896, Sara gained employment at the institution and became its superintendent in 1901.[37]

In 1901 Christian Fleetwood applied for a pension. In his application, he stated that he had total deafness in his left ear, likely the result of a "gunshot concussion." A "severe" hearing loss was noted in his right ear, a condition Fleetwood attributed to an ailment from his military service. Sadly, Fleetwood added that these situations negated his singing or speaking in public.[38]

Christian Fleetwood, seventy-four years old, passed away from heart disease September 28, 1914. His funeral services were held at St. Luke's Episcopal Church. Fleetwood's death was announced in two location of the September 30, 1914 issue of Washington D.C.'s *Evening Star*. In the "Death Record" section, under the heading of "Colored," a statement noted, "Christian A. Fleetwood, 74, 1419 Swann St. NW." The second mention of Christian Fleetwood's passing made a reference to his well-documented participation in civic activities. It proclaimed, "Members of the Frederick Douglass Relief Association are hereby notified of the death of Maj. Christian Fleetwood, late a member of the Frederick Douglass Relief Association." The second reference to Fleetwood noted the location of the funeral as well. [39]

Christian Fleetwood, soldier, editor, singer, and activist was buried in Harmony Cemetery in Washington, D. C. His Medal of Honor was presented to the Smithsonian National Museum of American History at the request of his daughter in 1948. That endowment made Fleetwood the first African American veteran to be honored within the Smithsonian structures.[40]

CHAPTER THIRTEEN

James Gardiner (Gardner) (1839-1905)

L ittle is known about the early life of James Daniel Gardiner. However, his surname is also recorded as Gardner. Evidence indicates Gardner was born a free man in Gloucester, Virginia, with one source indicating the specific date as being September 16, 1839.

His pre-war occupation has been noted as gathering and selling oysters.[1]

On September 15, 1863, Gardiner signed up for three years of service in the 2nd North Carolina Colored Volunteers. National Park Service records indicate that Gardiner entered service at Yorktown, Virginia. The unit he joined had been organized at New Bern, North Carolina and Portsmouth, Virginia as a portion of Brigadier General Edward Augustus Wild's African Brigade. General Wild was a medical doctor who had earned a reputation as a strong abolitionist. Wild had also been wounded in battle and had lost an arm to amputation.[2]

The 2nd North Carolina Colored Volunteers was renamed the 36th United States Colored Troops on February 8, 1864, and Gardiner was a member of Company I in that regiment. The National Park Service records that the 36th U.S.C.T. was then attached to the U. S. Forces, Norfolk and Portsmouth, Department of Virginia and North Carolina through April 1864. For the following two months, the 36th U.S.C.T. troops were members of the District of St. Mary's, Department of Virginia and North Carolina. Interesting, the 36th U.S.C.T. was unattached from June to August 1864. A subsequent assignment to the 2nd Brigade, 3rd Division, 18th Corps lasted from August to December 1864.[3]

Throughout the various alignments his compatriots and he faced, James Gardiner saw little action. The summer of 1864 was largely devoted to the task of guarding Confederate prisoners at Point Lookout, Maryland. The assignment to Federal General Benjamin

Butler's Army of the James in latter 1864 would forever impact Private Gardiner.[4]

The first significant engagement for James Gardiner took place at New Market Heights, also known as Chaffin's Farm, on September 29, 1864. Gardiner and his fellow regimental members began the battle as part of the reserves while Colonel Samuel A. Duncan's Third Brigade suffered horrific casualties while attacking the Confederate position. After Duncan's troops were pushed back, Brigadier General Charles Paine ordered Colonel Alonzo Draper, Gardiner's regimental commander, to move against the men in gray.[5]

Serving a reserve role at Chaffin's Farm, Gardiner and his compatriots were unable to see much of the battlefield due to a heavy fog. The sun eventually burned the fog from the area, clearly revealing the Confederate position against which the men of the 36th U.S.C.T. were to advance. Dead, dying, and wounded men in blue regularly marked the terrain Gardiner crossed.[6]

Colonel Alonzo Draper recorded the events that transpired in the minutes that followed. Draper wrote, "After passing about 300 yards through young pines, always under fire, we emerged upon the open plain about 800 yards from the enemy's works...the brigade charged with shouts, losing heavily. Within twenty or thirty yards of the rebel line we found a swamp which broke the charge...men had to wade the run or stream and reform on the bank."[7]

Draper recalled, "...men generally commenced firing, which made so much confusion that it was impossible to make the orders understood. Our men were falling by scores. All the officers were striving constantly to get the men forward. I passed frequently from the right to the left, urging every regimental commander to rally his men around the colors and charge."[8]

The Federals were able to successfully charge the Confederate stronghold. One of the primary reasons for the Federal achievement was credited to Gardiner, reportedly one of the first Federal troops to enter the Confederate works. During the assault, Gardiner encountered a Confederate officer who met his doom when Gardiner shot and stabbed him with a bayonet.[9]

A significant number of Gardiner's compatriots followed him into the Confederate stronghold where the opposing soldiers reportedly engaged in hand-to-hand combat. One historian remarked, "Black men with arms of iron fought Southern white soldiers...with desperate valor. In the end it was those who held the philosophy that black men were inferior...were driven from the field."[10]

The initial recognition for Gardiner's heroic actions came the day after the battle. At that time, Gardiner was promoted to the rank of sergeant.[11] More accolades lay in store for the man who rallied his fellow soldiers at Chaffin's Farm.

On April 6, 1865, Sergeant James Gardiner received the Medal of Honor for his deeds of September 29, 1864. Words of praise from General Benjamin Butler included, "Gardiner...in advance of his brigade, shot a rebel officer who was on the parapet rallying his men, and then ran him through with his bayonet." Gardiner also received the Butler Award, an honor Butler designed, funded, and selected for those he deemed worthy.[12]

His post-war experiences included him joining his regiment as it moved to Texas. Sadly, various poor choices on Gardiner's part created discipline problems for the Medal of Honor recipient. Due to what was reported as "incompetence and for being slovenly and dirty in his habit," Sergeant James Gardiner received a reduction in rank to private July 13, 1865.[13]

Private James Gardiner was jailed in Brazos Santiago, Texas on March 29, 1866. Approximately six months later, September 20, 1866, Gardiner, or Gardner, was discharged from the military. One Gardner historian has noted that the Medal of Honor recipient's military service was one that, "...started as a promising career [and] ended in disappointing obscurity."[14]

James Daniel Gardner served as a Catholic missionary after the war, and he lived in various locations, including Burlington and Ottumwa, Iowa during that time. Gardner was a resident of Clark's Summit, Pennsylvania when he passed away on September 29, 1905, the forty-first anniversary of his heroism at Chaffin's Farm. A headstone bearing the surname Gardner marks his grave in Calvary Crest Cemetery in Ottumwa, Iowa.[15]

On May 6, 2006, a monument was dedicated to James Daniel Gardner. Approximately 200 people attended the Gloucester, Virginia ceremony which focused on Gardner as a representative of the soldiers who fought for their country during the American Civil War. Reenactors from New Jersey, Delaware, Pennsylvania, Massachusetts, and Virginia participated in the event and depicted Confederate and Federal soldiers.[16] The fitting tribute to a hero epitomized the recognition many veterans of the American Civil War failed to duly receive.

CHAPTER FOURTEEN

James Harris
(1828-1898)

The biography of James H. Harris is among the least thorough of any Medal of Honor recipient. Even the wording on his Medal of Honor citation is brief and seemingly incomplete. While few details exist in relation to his exploits before, during, or after the American Civil War, James H. Harris and his heroic actions of September 29, 1864 warrant discussion.

Information from Arlington National Cemetery indicates Harris was born in St. Mary's County, Maryland. An estimated 700 of the 6,500 slaves in the Maryland county were recruited into service of the United States. Holding the vocation of a farmer, the thirty-six-year-old Harris entered the army February 14, 1864 in Great Mills, St. Mary's County, Maryland.[1]

Having enlisted in Company B of the 38th United States Colored Troops, Harris rose through the ranks quickly and became a sergeant September 10, 1864. He held that rank when he joined his fellow regimental members as they advanced against Confederate troops at Chaffin's Farm, or New Market Heights, on September 29, 1864.[2]

The Army of the James contained some 35,000 men in the XVIII and X Corps, as well as a cavalry division. Under the command of Major General Benjamin Butler, the troops were to spearhead an attack against Confederates in the vicinity of Petersburg. Fourteen African American soldiers, including James H. Harris, displayed acts of heroism in the ensuing action, earning each of them a Medal of Honor.[3]

In the ensuing attack, lasting approximately and hour and costing the Federal division about 800 casualties, a lack of coordinated efforts hampered the Federals. Harris was noted as performing a gallant act that earned him the highest military recognition.[4] Little additional insight into his actions exists.

On February 18, 1874, nine and a half years after his display of heroism, James H. Harris received the Medal of Honor. Harris, along with Private William Henry Barnes and 1st Sergeant Edward Ratcliff, was one of the three members of the 38th U. S. C. T. awarded the Medal of Honor for bravery during the American Civil War. Another display of the lack of information about Harris and his military activities is indicated in his Medal of Honor citation. The text simply states that the medal was awarded for "gallantry in the assault."[5]

Sergeant Harris spent nine months after New Market Heights recovering from wounds received in the battle. Harris remained in the military until January 25, 1867 when he was mustered out at Indianola, Texas. The National Park Service states that while no reason is provided, Harris had his rank reduced to that of private prior to his completion of service.[6]

James H. Harris spent his post-war years working as a carpenter in Washington, D. C. In addition to his earnings in that vocation, Harris was the recipient of a $12 monthly pension.[7]

Harris passed away January 28, 1898. His remains were interred in Section 27, Grave 985-H of Arlington National Cemetery. Erected March 4, 2012, monument in Lexington Park, St. Mary's County, Maryland honors Harris and William Barnes, as well as Joseph Hayden, the two African Americans and one white soldier who hailed from that location and won the Medal of Honor. An additional act of respect toward Harris rests in the fact that the Sgt. James H. Harris Camp #38 of the Sons of Union Veterans, based in Maryland, bears his name.[8]

CHAPTER FIFTEEN

Thomas Hawkins
(1840-1870)

The exact date Thomas Hawkins was born is not recorded, but 1840 is generally accepted as the year. Cincinnati, Ohio was the location of his birth, but by 1863 Hawkins was living in Philadelphia,

Pennsylvania.¹ No other information related to his pre-war activities exists.

The Ohio native became a member of the 6th United States Colored Troops in August 1863. At that point, Hawkins, who listed his pre-war employment as that of a plasterer, enlisted for a three-year period as a substitute for Passmore Henry, another Philadelphia resident. Hawkins was assigned to Company C of the regiment.²

Nineteen days after enlisting, Hawkins was promoted to the rank of sergeant-major. At that approximate point of his military career, Hawkins and the men of the 6th USCT were sent to Yorktown, Virginia. The unit remained in Yorktown until the spring of 1864.³

Sergeant Major Thomas Hawkins joined his regiment during its first engagement of the war, Petersburg, Virginia. During the June 15, 1864 action at Petersburg, a bullet hit Hawkins near the elbow and broke his arm. The wound resulted in Hawkins being hospitalized eight weeks. He was able to rejoin the 6th USCT at Dutch Gap on August 13, 1864.⁴

On September 29, 1864, Hawkins and members of the 6th USCT entered the battle of New Market Heights, or Chaffin's Farm, near 5:30 a.m. It has been noted that a thick fog met the blue-clad members of the 6th USCT "like a mantle of death" as they approached the Confederate earthworks near Richmond. The men of the 6th USCT "quickly ran into a torrent of musket and artillery fire that cut through their ranks and shredded the national and regimental colors..."⁵

In the ensuing events, the 6th USCT suffered a casualty rate of 57%. Sergeant Major Hawkins was among the wounded at New Market Heights as he received injuries to an arm, heart, and a foot.[6] The exact details involving his injury are sketchy.

What is known about Hawkins and his wounds centers upon a specific portion of the action at New Market Heights. Within minutes of the 6th USCT entering battle, the soldiers who carried the national flag and the regimental colors were wounded. First Sergeant Alexander Kelly grabbed the national colors, while Sergeant Major Hawkins and Lieutenant Nathan Edgerton secured the regimental flag. The banner contained the motto, "Freedom for All."[7]

Hawkins was wounded to the extent that his friend Christian Fleetwood noted, "...his recovery from these fearful wounds was deemed hopeless." However, Hawkins was able to recover from his wounds, but he was seriously crippled. The regimental surgeon proclaimed the injuries to be so severe that Sergeant Major Hawkins was two-thirds disabled. As a result, Hawkins received a disability discharge on May 20, 1865.[8]

For their actions at New Market Heights, a dozen black soldiers, including Christian Fleetwood, were awarded Medals of Honor April 6, 1865. Sergeant Major Thomas Hawkins was not among that number of recipients. Therefore, he began an appeal for his recognition.[9]

It took a significant amount of time and effort for Hawkins to receive his Medal of Honor. Major General Joseph Barr Kiddoo received a post-war correspondence from Hawkins, asking about the probability of Hawkins being awarded a Medal of Honor. Kiddoo evidently agreed, as he sought the War Department's approval.[10]

On February 8, 1870, Thomas Hawkins received the Medal of Honor. The award was reportedly hand-delivered to Hawkins. His citation partially read, "The President of the United States...takes pleasure in presenting the Medal of Honor to Sergeant Major Thomas R. Hawkins...for rescue of regimental colors."[11] His time of celebration would be short-lived.

Thomas Hawkins was either 29 or 30 when he passed away from the effects of cancer on February 28, 1870. There is some dispute about his exact cause of death, as consumption is another reason sometimes noted. That tragic event occurred less than three weeks after Hawkins received his Medal of Honor. His survivors included his wife and young son.[12]

A wonderful tribute to Hawkins came from fellow Medal of Honor recipient Christian Fleetwood. Two days after Hawkins passed, Fleetwood wrote, "His death leaves a void in the hearts of his associates that will never be filled..."[13] Thus was the positive impression Hawkins gave in his short life.

Although he was originally interred in Columbian Harmony Cemetery in D. C., that burial ground eventually closed. In 1960, his remains, along with an estimated 37,000 others, were moved to National Harmony Park Cemetery in Maryland. In the mid-1990s a memorial plaque was placed at his grave.[14]

Another memorial to the Medal of Honor heroism of Thomas Hawkins took place during a June 24, 2013 unveiling. On that date, artist Don Troiani premiered artwork entitled *Three Medal of Honor*, a painting that depicts the actions of Hawkins, Lieutenant Nathan Edgerton, and First Sergeant Alexander Kelly as the trio earned the prestigious honor.[15]

CHAPTER SIXTEEN

Alfred Hilton
(1840-1864)

Alfred Hilton was born in the Gravel Hill, Maryland community, an area known as a haven for free blacks. It has been noted that the location is ironic in that Hilton was born free, while slavery was "accepted and protected" in the county of his birth. Some records indicate his year of birth as 1842 while others record the year as being as early as 1837. His parents, former slaves, had a total of fourteen children whom they raised in Gravel Hill, a post on the Underground Railroad. Other nearby towns such as Havre de Grace, Berkley and Kalmia, all sister settlements in Harford County, Maryland, also provided safety for runaway slaves.[1]

By 1860, Harford County recorded almost 3,700 free blacks as residents. That number constituted some sixteen percent of the county's population and twice the total of enslaved persons, 1,800, in the county. The total Harford County population was noted as 23,415.[2]

Additional records indicate that Alfred B. Hilton was living in the Hopewell, Maryland area, near Havre de Grace when the American Civil War began. His parents had purchased fourteen acres from John and Sarah Charshee for $320 in the last full year before the war. The Hilton parents, in their 60s by the time they acquired the farm, maintained a household that served as the residence of Alfred, four of his brothers, and a sister. A 40-year-old African American woman named Hannah Jones also resided with the Hilton family. All of the Hilton family members were listed as illiterate.[3]

There appears to be little explanation and only conjecture as to what had happened to other members of the Hilton family who were recognized in the 1850 census. Listed as 6, 7, and 14 years-old at the time of that count, Eliza, Ann, and Alice, were not living with the Hilton parents when the 1860 census was conducted. Edward and Henry, two of Alfred's brothers, were also unaccounted for in the 1860 census.[4]

Aaron and Henry Hilton, two of Alfred Hilton's brothers, both noted as freedmen, were members of the 4th U. S. Colored Troops by August 1863. Over two hundred men from Harford County joined the U.S.C.T.; twenty-six served in the same regiment as Aaron and Henry Hilton.[5]

Alfred Hilton, listed as a farmer on his parents' land possession, also enlisted in Company H of the 4th U.S. Colored Troops August 11, 1863. The 4th U.S.C.T. was a segregated unit under the command of white officers. Historians differ as to the exact location of

Hilton's enlistment, as the event is noted as having taken place in Havre de Grace or at Baltimore. Listed as age 21, Hilton was noted as standing five feet, ten and a half inches tall when he entered the U. S. Army.[6]

Hilton's height was alternately stated in another document that stated as over six feet tall. In addition, Christian Fleetwood, a man who would later join Hilton as earning a Medal of Honor, recalled Hilton was a "magnificent specimen of manhood...splendidly proportioned."[7]

Alfred Hilton experienced considerable combat from June through September 1864 as he carried the United States flag in engagements in the vicinities of Richmond and Petersburg.[8] Those battles and the related experiences for Alfred Hilton soon gave way as the 4th U.S.C.T. prepared for upcoming action at New Market Heights, a location situated east of Richmond.

During the September 29, 1864 action at New Market Heights, or Chaffin's Farm, Hilton carried the flag and served as the color guard's sergeant. When another soldier, carrying the regimental flag, was wounded, Sergeant Hilton took the second banner from the incapacitated man. Approaching the Confederate fortifications, Hilton was shot through the leg.[9]

Struggling from the severe leg wound, Sergeant Alfred Hilton allegedly yelled, "Boys, save the colors!" As those words escaped his mouth, Hilton was said to have passed the standards to two fellow soldiers, Sergeant Major Christian Fleetwood and Private Charles Veale, preventing the flags from hitting the ground.[10]

Praise for Sergeant Hilton and his actions were quickly exclaimed. General Benjamin Butler issued an

October 11, 1864 order that stated, "...Hilton, color-sergeant...the bearer of the national colors, when the color-sergeant with the regimental standard fell beside him, seized the standard, struggled forward with both colors..." Butler's commendation for Hilton continued, "...disabled by a severe wound at the enemy's inner line...when on the ground he showed that his thoughts were for the colors and not for himself. He has a special medal for gallantry, and will have his warrant as first sergeant."[11]

Sergeant Alfred Hilton's severe wound caused his right leg to be amputated below the knee. The injury and the subsequent suffering proved insurmountable obstacles for the young soldier, as he died in the segregated Fort Monroe hospital October 21, 1864. His remains were interred at Hampton National Cemetery in Hampton, Virginia. Hilton's grave in located in Section E-1231 of the cemetery.[12]

On April 6, 1865, approximately eight months after Hilton's death, Sergeant Alfred B. Hilton became a posthumous recipient of the Medal of Honor. His citation read, in part, "...for extraordinary heroism on 29 September 1864...Sergeant Hilton seized the Color and carried it forward, together with the national standard, until disabled at the enemy's inner line." Interestingly, Fleetwood and Veale, the two men who took the flags from the wounded Sergeant Hilton, also earned the Medal of Honor.[13]

Sadly, the precise location Hilton's Medal of Honor is unknown. Not a single descendant of his siblings is aware of the medal's whereabouts. Additionally, Alfred Hilton never married. As an added mystery into the preservation of Hilton's memory, there are no known photographs of him.[14] Interestingly, not all is lost in regard to the preservation of Alfred Hilton's legacy.

A Maryland historical marker, located northwest of Havre de Grace, stands along Gravel Hill Road and in the parking lot of Alfred B. Hilton Park. The 12-acre park was dedicated Memorial Day 2002, and it had previously been known as Gravel Hill Park. The address of the park is 4020 Gravel Hill Road, approximately one-quarter mile east of Paradise Road, Maryland 462. The office hours for the park are from 8 a.m. to 4:30 p.m. Monday through Friday. The marker, situated near the former village of Gravel Hill, provides insight into his life and his actions related to the Medal of Honor.[15]

Another act of appreciation for Sergeant Alfred B. Hilton took place November 9, 2017. Found a few miles south of the park, the Route 22/Interstate 95 four-lane overpass was named in Hilton's honor. The legislation to have to the recognition realized was the co-sponsored legislation of Harford State Senator Robert Cassillly and Del. Mary Ann Lisanti and met the approval of the Maryland General Assembly. The legislative body authorized the Maryland Transportation Authority to carry out the designation of the Alfred B. Hilton Memorial Bridge.[16]

A November 9, 2017 article relayed more of the activities associated with the dedication of the bridge. Maryland Transportation Deputy Secretary James F. Ports, Jr. was quoted as saying, "In a time when sacrifices are often forgotten, I am humbled by the opportunity to stand here today and honor a true American hero. His charge into battle and the sacrifice that he made will be forever memorialized for all to see." Another event speaker, Kevin C. Reigrut, Executive Director of the MDTA, added, "Sgt. Hilton's story is a fascinating and shining example of Maryland's finest. What an honor it is to share his legacy and his story of bravery." Reigrut added, "It was in recognizing his sacrifice that we gather today to honor and celebrate his life."[17]

Hilton's dedication to his beliefs and convictions are far from unique. However, the conditions under which he lived and served are clearly described in a 2000 issue of the *Harford Historical Bulletin*. Historian James Chrismer penned, "Hilton's life was characterized by poverty, illiteracy, insecurity, discrimination, obscurity, and an untimely death and burial far from family and loved ones."[18] Sadly, this set of words related to Hilton could be applied to a large number of his fellow soldiers in the American Civil War and those other conflicts in which the nation he served has been involved.

CHAPTER SEVENTEEN

Milton Holland
(1844-1910)

Milton Murray Holland was reportedly born in Austin, Texas August 1, 1844. Some sources signal Carthage, Texas as the location of Holland's birth. However, there is doubt as to the exact date of his birth. Other noteworthy facets related to his birth rest in the parentage of Milton Holland. His parents were originally recorded as John and Matilda Holland. His mother, Matilda, was a slave whose owner was Spearman "Major" Holland. Spearman Holland had a half-brother named Bird Holland. A great deal of evidence points toward Bird Holland being Milton Holland's father as well as six other children of Matilda. Due to his generally-accepted parentage, Milton Holland was regarded as "a fair-skinned" individual.[1]

Bird Holland had served in the Mexican War during which he held the rank of captain in the Second Regiment, Texas Mounted Volunteers. A disease, likely cholera, resulted in Captain Bird Holland resigning on August 8, 1846. Sadly, Kemp Holland, a brother of Bird Holland, died in camp during the war. Bird Holland eventually held the post of Texas secretary of state and signed the state's new constitution that made it a member of the Confederacy.[2]

In the 1850s, Bird Holland managed to purchase Milton and Milton's brothers, William and James, from Spearman "Major" Holland. In turn, Milton Holland was sent to Albany Enterprise Academy, also known as the Albany Manual Labor Academy, in Ohio. That educational facility was under the direction of abolitionists and free African Americans and had been established in 1847. A declaration from an 1849 article in *The Saturday Visiter* noted the academy's educational philosophy in stating that the with combining studies and manual labor, the founders of the institution desired to, "...rebuke the withering spirit of caste, and as far as our influence extends, make all forms of useful industry respectable, and furnish community with practical men and women instead of mere theorists." At approximately the same time the Holland brothers enrolled at the academy, shares valued at $25 were sold to individuals deemed as possessing "good moral character."[3]

In addition to seeking better education for his children, Bird Holland had married Matilda Rust, the slave mother of James, Milton, and William, on October 1, 1857. Sadly, Matilda passed away the following year.[4]

In the days following the onset of the American Civil War, Milton Holland attempted to enlist into the service of the United States. It was written that Milton Holland was "among the first boys of his school to throw down his books and respond to the call of his country." Holland was denied, due to his young age, but he managed to gain employment as a shoemaker for the Quartermaster Department and was an aide-de-camp for Colonel Nelson Van Vorhes, an officer who commanded the 3rd, 18th, and 92nd Ohio Infantry Regiments.[5]

Milton Holland allegedly learned the trade of making shoes while enrolled at Albany Manual Labor University. Indications also exist that Milton Holland and his older brother William possibly enlisted in the Attucks' Guards, a group of black soldiers named for American Independence casualty Crispus Attucks. The Attucks' Guards, carrying a flag which the women of Albany made, marched to the Ohio governor's mansion where they offered their services, but that proposition was declined.[6]

Holland's father, Bird Holland, left his position as Texas secretary of state in November 1861 and joined the Confederate Army. Bird Holland soon held the rank of major in the Twenty-second Texas Infantry. At the age of forty-nine, Bird Holland was killed April 8, 1864 while leading his regiment in the battle of Mansfield, Louisiana. His body was returned to Austin, Texas for burial and was interred in Oakwood Cemetery next to Matilda Holland's grave. Although Bird Holland had served in the Texas State House and as state secretary, any possible official portrait and/or records related to those posts were lost when the Texas Capitol burned in 1881. Family members also failed to save diaries that belonged to Holland.[7]

Following Secretary of War Edwin Stanton's June 1862 agreement to allow black men to enlist, Milton Holland joined the 11th Ohio Militia Infantry in Athens, Ohio. At the time of his three-year enlistment, Holland was described as eighteen years old, five feet eight inches tall, with a yellow complexion, black hair, and brown eyes. Records note while Holland was at the Athens County Fairgrounds, he managed to recruit one hundred forty-nine African-American males and raised what would become Company C of the 5th United States Colored Troops.[8]

The following year, the regiment was mustered into the service of the United States as the Fifth U. S. Colored Troops. Milton Holland's records at Arlington National Cemetery state that the activity took place June 22, 1863 at Delaware, Ohio.[9]

A witness to the group of which Milton Holland was a member described Holland by writing, "He was a young colored Texan...by nature a soldier. He smelt battle from afar, and was ready at the shortest warning to engage in deadly conflict...a young person of remarkable native intelligence...as to win the largest respect and confidence..."[10]

As a member of the 5th United States Colored Troops, Milton Holland was under the command of General Benjamin Butler. Having served as a drillmaster, Holland, along with his comrades, soon saw action in the North Carolina swamps. It was noted that the 5th United States Colored Troops spent significant efforts "capturing forage and emancipating slaves." Butler justified those actions based upon his interpretation of the Emancipation Proclamation.[11]

Milton Holland recorded the exploits of his group in remarking, "...regiment...has been in active service for three months...has been in one engagement. The men stood nobly and faced the cowardly foe when they were hid in the swamp..." Additional praise for his regimental peers included, "They stood like men, and when ordered to charge, went in with a yell, and came out victorious, losing four killed and several wounded..."[12]

Soon promoted to first sergeant of Company C in the 5th U. S. Colored Troops, Milton Holland served with the James River fleet as it advanced toward Richmond. Milton Holland and his fellow regimental members spent the spring of 1864 conducting raids near Richmond and liberating captives from Libby Prison. Another raid led to the group assisting General Hugh Kilpatrick who was in the midst of a Confederate siege. Although not involved in the action at the Crater, Holland and his fellow company members were ordered to make an attack and "struck the first blow at Petersburg" by capturing the Confederate flag, the signal station, and the officers who were at the station. In time, Milton Holland attained the rank of sergeant-major, the highest rank an African-American could attain at the time.[13]

In late September 1864, Sergeant-Major Milton Holland joined his comrades in hand-to-hand combat at Chaffin's Farm or New Market Heights, Virginia. In the ensuing struggle, every white officer was wounded or killed, and Sergeant-Major Holland joined other black soldiers, leading the remaining Federal troops advancing against the Confederates. The resulting victory eventually enabled the Federals to move closer toward Richmond.[14]

Sergeant-Major Holland was wounded in the charge against the Rebel position, but he managed to successfully lead his men in a heroic charge, having never left the field. A field commission to the rank of captain awaited Holland. However, the U. S. War Department refused to acknowledge the increase in rank due to Milton Holland's race. An offer from Ohio Governor David Tod would have placed Holland into a different regiment with the rank of captain. The major stipulation in that scenario was for Milton Holland, a light-skinned African American, to claim his identity as a white man. Milton Holland refused to deny his race.[15] The efforts of Sergeant-Major Holland and his fellow-Federal soldiers would not otherwise go unnoticed.

After his heroic actions at Chaffin's Farm, Milton Holland received praise from General Benjamin Butler. On October 11, 1864, General Benjamin Butler noted the actions of Sergeant Major Milton Holland. Butler stated, "Milton M. Holland...Fifth U.S. Colored Troops, commanding Company C...left in command, all...company officers being killed or wounded...led them gallantly and meritoriously through the day. For these services...the commanding general will cause a special medal to be struck..." Butler then offered his endorsement for a unique recognition to be directed toward Holland, James Bronson, Robert Pinn, and Powhatan Beaty. General Butler concluded, "...the commanding general will cause a special medal to be struck in honor of these gallant colored soldiers."[16]

The Butler Medal, made from Tiffany silver, depicted a black soldier advancing upon an enemy parapet. The medal was originally identified as the Colored Troop Medal. It has been stated that this was the only award of its type designated for black soldiers.[17]

Sergeant-Major Holland and his mates spent January 1865 conducting patrol duty. The primary area of the North Carolina lowlands near Fort Fisher. Through their actions, an untold number of slaves were freed, and Confederate guerilla fighters captured.[18]

Milton Holland's actions at Chaffin's Farm resulted in him receiving the Congressional Medal of Honor April 6, 1865, only three days before the Appomattox surrender. The text for Sergeant-Major Milton Holland's Medal of Honor citation stated, in part, "Took command of Company C, after all the officers had been killed or wounded, and gallantly led it." In earning this recognition, Holland became the first Texan to do so.[19]

Milton Holland was at Bennett Place, North Carolina April 26, 1865. That day witnessed Confederate Joseph Johnston surrendering to General William Sherman. Information indicates Holland found out about

President Lincoln's assassination while at Bennett Place.[20]

As well as serving his country, Milton Holland dedicated himself to African American activism. A portion of one of his war letters stated, "There is a brighter day coming for the colored man, and he must sacrifice home, comforts if necessary, to speed the coming of the glorious day."[21]

Sergeant-Major Milton Holland was mustered out of service September 20, 1865. That reentry into civilian life took place at Carolina City, North Carolina. Milton Holland also married Virginia Dickey in Columbus, Ohio October 24, 1865. There are no indications that Milton Holland ever made a post-war visit to his birth state of Texas. From the time of their marriage until April 1866, Milton and Virginia Holland lived in Columbus. From April 1866 through October of the same year, the couple lived in Albany and then returned to Columbus for a period of approximately three years.[22]

His brother William did return to Texas, attended Oberlin College, served in the state legislature, and helped create Prairie View Normal, the first African American college in Texas. William Holland also assisted in forming The Deaf, Dumb, and Blind Institute for Colored Youth; he served as superintendent of that establishment for eleven years.[23]

Milton Holland's post-war activities included him moving to Washington, D.C. While in the nation's capital he held a job in the Auditor Office as a clerk in the U. S. Treasury Department and earned $1,200 per year. Holland eventually served as the chief of collections for the Sixth District. Holland's annual salary soon reached

$2,000. In addition, Milton Holland formed Alpha Insurance Company, an early African-American-owned insurance company. Having graduated from Howard University in 1872, Milton Holland opened a law practice, largely focused upon real estate issues, and he engaged in Republican politics. Holland also secured offices in two black-owned banks, Capital Saving Bank and the Industrial Building and Savings Company. An individual familiar with Milton Holland's life recalled, "He is positive and business-like in his methods, quick and accurate in his mastery of details, untiring in his energy and fearless in his courage."[24]

Spearman "Major" Holland gave his plantation to his former slaves when the American Civil War concluded. Spearman Holland deemed this to be the correct step for him to take as the slaves had worked and harvested the parcels during their times of bondage. Spearman Holland made his post-war home in Carthage, Texas and died in 1872.[25]

Milton and Virginia Holland lived with their daughter in the ensuing years. Their home was described as a, "large, beautiful frame structure, modeled after the plan of a French villa, with...spacious lawns surrounding the entire home." Its located was noted as "...on Howard University Hill, commanding a fine view of the beautiful park...nicely furnished, and the library is well filled with a choice selection of the best works of the best authors." A more personal aspect added was, "His estimable wife and daughter preside over their home with a charm of manners that make it the social rendezvous of their many friends..."[26]

That 1889 statement regarding Milton Holland's wife and daughter leads to a mystery. In 1906, Holland reported to the Bureau of Pensions that he had no living children. Sadly, the cause of his daughter's death is unknown.[27]

Milton's Holland's quest to receive a pension from the federal government met with difficulty. It appears that he was initially challenged to prove his discharge was honorable. Holland made citations that impaired vision and deafness were disabilities he possessed when applying for the pension. He eventually succeeded in securing a pension of $12 per month. In 1902, Holland and his wife moved to Silver Springs, Maryland.[28]

Milton Holland, at the age of sixty-five, died of a heart attack May 15, 1910 at his farm near Silver Springs, Maryland. On May 18, 1910, Sergeant-Major Milton Holland was buried in Section 23 of Arlington National Cemetery. Holland's pension was passed to his widow who died September 18, 1915.[29]

On November 11, 2013, Veterans Day, a historical marker was dedicated at the Athens, Ohio Fairgrounds. The marker denotes the location where Milton Holland recruited men who later served in the 5th U. S. Colored Infantry Regiment. Several speakers and reenactors, including one portraying Milton Holland. The marker's sponsors were the Townsend 108 Sons of Union Veterans of the Civil War Camp with financial assistance from the Athens Foundation.[30]

CHAPTER EIGHTEEN

Miles James
(1829-1871)

Miles James, destined to earn the Medal of Honor for his heroism at Chaffin's Farm, Virginia, was born in 1829. The exact date appears to be unknown, but evidence points to the likely location as Virginia Beach City, Virginia.[1]

Indications are that James was raised in Prince Anne County, Virginia where he worked as a laborer and farmer. In 1863, he decided to join a company of African American troops that Federal Major General Edward Wild had raised.[2] Thus began the military service of one of the many heroes of the American Civil War.

At the time of his November 16, 1863 enlistment in the 36th U. S. C. T., formerly known as the 2nd North Carolina Colored Infantry Volunteers, James was noted as being a thirty-four-year-old farmer. Additional information records he was five feet seven inches in height with a black complexion.[3]

A strong indication of the extraordinary qualities of leadership, consistent ability to be present for duty, and/or exemplary conduct Miles James possessed are indicated in his service record. On February 15, 1864, less than three months after his enlistment, James was promoted to the rank of corporal.[4]

The first taste of combat for Corporal Miles James took place in North Carolina. Confederate guerillas attacked Federal troops, enabling James to "see the elephant," a term used for soldiers who experienced combat. Engagements at Wilson's Wharf, Suffolk, and Petersburg created what one historian deemed as a "battle-hardened, well-respected unit."[5]

September 30, 1864 found Corporal Miles James and his fellow brigade members at Chapin's Farm and under the command of Colonel Alonzo Draper. The unit was assigned the task of advancing toward a strong Confederate position.[6] The assault would have devastating physical effects for James as well as military and personal glory.

As Corporal James moved within thirty yards of the Confederate breastworks, he was shot in the upper left arm. A projectile struck and shattered the bone, rendering the limb useless. Proving his physical endurance under duress, Corporal James continued loading and discharging his rifle while using only one arm. In addition, Corporal James maintained his composure and urged his compatriots to advance into an eventual Federal victory.[7]

A field amputation was conducted following the engagement, with Corporal Miles James receiving recovery care at Fort Monroe. The severity of his wound would have likely enabled Corporal James to reenter the civilian life. However, on February 4, 1865, Colonel Alonzo Draper wrote a letter pleading that the opposite be done for Corporal James.[8]

Colonel Draper noted that James had made a request to remain in the 36th U. S. C. T., and Draper asked for the plea to be granted. In part, Colonel Draper penned, "I would most respectfully urge that...be granted...He is one of the bravest men I ever saw; and is in every respect a model soldier." Draper continued in writing, "He is worth more with his single arm, than half a dozen ordinary men. Being a Sergeant, he will have very little occasion...to use a musket. He could be Sergt. of my Provost Guard or Hd. Qtr. Guard..." It appears James and Draper's wishes were approved, as Colonel Draper issued a special order on April 18, 1865 that provided James with a sergeant's sword in lieu of a musket.[9]

Approximately three weeks after the battle of Chapin's or Chaffin's Farm, also known as Fort Harrison, Virginia, Miles James was recognized in an order from General Benjamin Butler. The October 11, 1864 statement proclaimed that Corporal Miles James of the Thirty-sixth U. S. Colored Troops, "...after having his arm so badly mutilated that immediate amputation was necessary, loaded and discharged his piece with one hand, and urged his men forward; this within thirty yards of the enemy's works. He has a medal and a sergeant's warrant."[10]

Less than a year after joining the military at Norfolk, Virginia, Corporal Miles James received the

Congressional Medal of Honor. The presentation took place April 6, 1865.[11]

The Medal of Honor citation for Miles James not only stated that the President took pleasure in presenting the distinction to Miles, but it also gave a brief explanation of his September 30, 1864 actions at Chaffin's Farm. The citation read, "Having had his arm mutilated, making immediate amputation necessary, Corporal James loaded and discharged his piece with one hand and urged his men forward; this within 30 yards of the enemy's works."[12]

Sergeant Miles James was given a discharge October 13, 1865. At that time, his regiment was serving the remainder of its enlistment at Brazos Springs, Texas.[13] Sadly, little additional information exists in relation to the post-war life of Miles James.

On August 28, 1871, almost seven years after receiving the Congressional Medal of Honor, James Miles passed away in Norfolk City, Virginia. Due to the uncertainty of his birthdate, it is left to conjecture as to whether his age at time of his death was forty-one or forty-two. Some sources state that the location of his burial is unknown, but findagrave.com, a website noted for exploring such historical aspects, claims the gravesite of James Miles is in the Sgt. March Corprew Family Cemetery in Chesapeake City, Virginia.[14]

In May 2013, a marker was placed in a small cemetery in Bells Mill, Virginia for the purpose of honoring the services of Miles James and other African Americans who earned the Medal of Honor during the American Civil War. Praising James, E. Curtis Alexander, a representative of the Chesapeake- based United States

Colored Troops Descendants said, "He was quite a man. I can't even imagine what he went through, or how he did what he did."[15]

CHAPTER NINETEEN

Alexander Kelly
(1840-1907)

Medal of Honor recipient Alexander Kelly was born April 1840. Dispute exists as to whether the exact date was April 5 or 7, but Saltsburg, Conemaugh Township, Indiana County, Pennsylvania appears to be the regarded location of his birth. Information from Census and Service Records indicates Kelly was a "mulatto" and had "light skin." In addition, records show that he was short of stature, standing five feet three inches in height.[1]

Alexander Kelly and his siblings were orphaned by 1850. Fortunately, the Kelly children were able to live with and uncle named David Kelly, a "salt boiler" by profession. David Kelly likely had a wife, a lady named Nancy, who was described as "keeping house" for the family[2] and who probably provided well-needed maternal affection toward the youngsters.

Alexander Kelly's pre-war vocation was a coal miner in Western Pennsylvania. That area was rich in salt deposits due to the Conemaugh River's formation in the vicinity.[3]

On August 24, 1863, Alexander Kelly enlisted in the 6th United States Colored Troops as a substitute for his brother in Allegheny City, Pennsylvania. At least one source shows that the entry into service took place as early as April 1863. His training took place at Camp William Penn, an establishment noted as "the first and largest Federal camp" that indoctrinated approximately 11,000 African American soldiers during the Civil War era.[4]

Under the command of Colonel John Ames, Alexander Kelly and his fellow members of the 6th U. S. C. T. marched in the streets of Philadelphia before making their way to combat. The early activities of the unit included service at Fortress Monroe and Yorktown in Virginia as well as taking part in capturing a Confederate post near Petersburg. Kelly moved with his comrades to the James River where they served fortification duty at Dutch Gap. The water in the area was polluted, and this fact sickened and killed a large number of the men in the 6th U. S. C. T. During this phase of his service, Alexander Kelly was promoted to the rank of sergeant.[5]

On September 29, 1864, the 6th U. S. C. T. was at Chaffin's Farm, an engagement also known as New Market Heights and Laurel Hill. Sergeant Alexander Kelly and approximately three hundred fifty other Federals advanced against a Confederate position with veteran Texas occupants under the leadership of Colonel Frederick Bass. In the initial charge, members of the color guard and numerous combatants fell from the "very intense firing."[6]

Although injured, Lieutenant Frederick Meyer took the fallen colors and moved toward the Confederate position. Another officer, Captain Edgerton, wrote, "I took it...and pushed forward to bring up the colors to their proper place. I sheathed my sword, took the flag with its broken staff and reached the abatis." Sergeant Alexander Kelly then took the flag from Edgerton and performed the heroic action that led to his earning the Medal of Honor.[7]

The citation for First Sergeant Alexander Kelly's Medal of Honor, presented April 6, 1865, stated, "Gallantly seized the colors, which had fallen near the enemy's lines of abatis, raised them, and rallied the men at a time of confusion and in a place of the greatest danger."[8]

Sergeant Alexander Kelly was mustered out of service with his company in Wilmington, North Carolina

September 20, 1865. He managed to secure the receipt of a monthly pension of $8; that amount was eventually increased to $12. Whether from his military action or otherwise, period records show that Alexander Kelly had "permanent marks" described as "a hole in his cheek, a lump over his eyes, and a scar on his back."[9]

Alexander Kelly married a lady named Victoria after the war; conflicting stories exist in relation to the number of children that they had. One modern source states the Kelly couple had a son named William. Alexander Kelly was eventually employed as a coal miner and lived in Coutlersville, Pennsylvania. There is information that the couple cared for orphans.[10]

Alexander and Victoria Kelly moved to the Pittsburgh East End by the early 1890's. Sadly, Victoria died in 1898. It appears that the Medal of Honor recipient was a stable watchman after 1900. William, his son, became a music teacher. Keeping in touch with others who served in the American Civil War, Alexander Kelly was a member of the Colonel Robert G. Shaw Grand Army of the Republic, Post 206.[11]

Alexander Kelly passed away June 19, 1907. The sixty-seven-year-old was buried next to his wife in Saint Peters Cemetery, on Lemington Avenue, in Pittsburgh, Pennsylvania. Kelly's grave is located in Division 3, Grave 13. A Medal of Honor grave memorial makes the location and recalls Alexander Kelly's military exploits.[12]

The heroic actions of Alexander Kelly, as well as those of Nathan Edgerton and Thomas Hawkins are depicted in artist Don Troiani's painting *Three Medals of Honor*. The artwork made its debut in 2013 at the Union League in Philadelphia.[13]

CHAPTER TWENTY

John Lawson
(1937-1919)

John Henry Lawson was born June 16, 1837. The location of his birth is usually regarded as Philadelphia, Pennsylvania. One Lawson biographer stated that Lawson was a slave at birth. The next major recorded aspect of John Lawson's life is that he served on the *U.S.S. Hartford* during the American Civil War.[1]

U.S.S. Hartford was built at Harrison Loring, Boston, in 1859. The wooden-hull screw sloop measured two hundred twenty-five feet long and had served as the flagship of the East India Squadron while it provided security for American interests in Asia. During the American Civil War, *Hartford* was fitted out in Philadelphia before serving as Flag Officer David Farragut's West Gulf Blockading Squadron's flagship. Action at locations such as New Orleans, Baton Rouge, Natchez, and New Orleans followed. The ship made its way toward Mobile, Alabama in June 1864.[2]

At this point, the history of John Lawson's life enters another stage of mystery. There is only conjecture as to exactly when John Lawson enlisted in the United States Navy and became a crewman on *Hartford*. One suggestion is that his entry into the navy occurred when the ship was in Philadelphia, and Lawson seized the opportunity to enlist. Another theory is John Lawson joined the U. S. Navy in New York as late as December 1863. A modern historian offered, "It is not known whether Lawson...had a maritime background; perhaps he...was experienced in dockside work but had yet to set said aboard a ship." Lastly, Lawson's height was recalled as five-feet eight inches, while his eyes were noted as grey in color. Interestingly both light and dark complexions were used in his description.[3]

On August 5, 1864, John Lawson was serving as a Landsman aboard *Hartford* in Mobile Bay, Alabama, a location one history professor exclaimed was "...the last remaining port on the Confederate Gulf Coast...cotton goes out...military goods and supplies come back." The designation of Landsman was reserved for recruits who had little or no previous experience on water. It was typical for a male joining the Navy to do so as a Landsman with the potential to advance to Ordinary Seaman, followed with the title of Seaman, and have the possibility of becoming a specialist in carpentry, gunnery, machinery, or other areas. His training was to serve as an ammunition handler in a six-man crew; that individual delivered live shells to gunners.[4]

The *U.S.S. Hartford* had two 20-pound Parrott rifles, two 12-pound guns, and twenty smoothbore Dahlgren guns. Four monitors and fourteen wooden ships composed Farragut's Federal fleet as it readied for an engagement against the Confederate ironclad *Tennessee*. At 8:45 a.m., *Tennessee* began its attack against Farragut's vessel.[5]

Confederate shells exploded near John Lawson, but witnesses said the sailor continued carrying out his duties. One historian wrote, "...an enemy shell struck the berth deck where Lawson and the rest of the ammunition team were stationed. The exploding shell either wounded or killed every man in the unit. Lawson...was seriously injured...and thrown violently..." Another added, "John Lawson...stunned...wounded, there are dead men on top of him...he gets up and continues passing the much-needed ammunition..." The tenacity John Lawson was capable of exhibiting is explained in the final recollection of the incident, "...recovering his senses...Lawson immediately returned to the shell-whip to resume his duties. His fellow sailors begged him to go below deck for medical treatment, but he steadfastly refused."[6]

On December 31, 1864, John Lawson received the Medal of Honor for his actions at Mobile. Lawson was one of a dozen men, four of whom were African American, who earned the Medal of Honor for heroism at Mobile.[7]

A portion of John Lawson's Medal of Honor citation stated, "Wounded in the leg and thrown violently against the side of the ship when an enemy shell killed or wounded the 6-man crew as the shell whipped on the berth deck, Lawson, upon regaining his composure, promptly returned to his station and, although urged to go below for treatment, steadfastly continued his duties throughout the remainder of the action."[8]

Upon his December 1864 end of service in the United States Navy, John Lawson returned to Philadelphia. His reported civilian vocation was that of a vendor or a huckster, an individual involved in door-to-door sales and who was considered "a less than honorable dealer." Lawson also reportedly "took up with" a lady named Mary Ann; the couple were noted as having children before separating in 1868.[9]

Other post-war activities which John Lawson pursued included him working as a cook and waiter in 1865. In 1870, Lawson was described as a Delmonico Society member. Lawson was recalled as owning a barber shop in 1892. That same year Lawson was approved for a pension of $4 per month due to his gunshot wound in the right leg and "affliction of head." In 1892, Lawson's Philadelphia address was listed as 602

Lombard Street, but he moved to 1334 Pearl Street in 1902.[10]

Eighty-one-year-old John Lawson passed away in Philadelphia, Pennsylvania May 3, 1919. Family members arranged for him to be buried at Mount Peace Cemetery in Lawnside, Camden County, New Jersey, a predominately African American community. Sadly, a lack of proper care and the effects of time led to his tombstone deteriorating beyond recognition. The cemetery office later suffered a fire that destroyed the location's map and burial records. Therefore, the exact site of John Lawson's grave is unknown. A new headstone was dedicated April 24, 2004 in Lawson's honor. It was placed in the area of the cemetery where over seventy veterans of the American Civil War are known to have been interred.[11]

John Lawson's name, as well as other black Naval Medal of Honorees, does not appear on the African American Civil War Memorial in Washington, D. C. A visitor recalled, "...names on the memorial are organized in alphabetical order within their regiments...One of the purposes of alphabetical order is to create equality, and that is the result here."[12]

As for the *Hartford*, the ship was decommissioned August 20, 1926. The guns were removed from the illustrious warship and sold for scrap metal. The vessel sank in her Norfolk, Virginia berth November 20, 1956. Towed to an abandoned wharf "and ripped to pieces," the remaining lower holds and keel were "soaked with inflammables and burned."[13]

CHAPTER TWENTY-ONE

James Mifflin
(1839-?)

James Mifflin was born in Richmond, Virginia in 1839. No information about his formative years is known to exist. The first certain information rests in his enlistment in the United States Navy and his assignment as an engineer's cook aboard the *U. S. S. Brooklyn*.[1]

The *Brooklyn* had been launched in 1858 and was commissioned January 26, 1859. The ship, serving under Admiral Farragut, spent the majority of the American Civil War as a member of the Gulf Coast Blockading Force. As such, the vessel saw action at New Orleans, Vicksburg, Pensacola, and Mobile Bay. It is uncertain at what point James Mifflin joined the crew.[2]

Mifflin's performance during the Battle of Mobile Bay, Alabama, on August 5, 1864, proved to be significant. By that point, the ship had two 100-pound muzzle loading rifles, two 60-pound muzzle loading rifles, twenty 9-inch smoothbores, and two 12-pound howitzers. Despite this heavy armament, Confederate shells struck the *Brooklyn,* and reportedly "cleared his shipmates" in the ensuing minutes.[3] At that point, James Mifflin exhibited his heroic actions.

Mifflin's Medal of Honor citation states, "...during...attacks against Fort Morgan, rebel gunboats, and the ram *Tennessee*...Stationed in the immediate vicinity of the shell whips, which were twice cleared of men by bursting shell, Mifflin remained steadfast at his post." The impact of Mifflin's conduct was noted in the citation's closing remarks, "...and performed his duties in the powder division throughout the furious action which resulted in the surrender of the prize ram *Tennessee* and in the damaging and destruction of batteries at Fort Morgan."[4]

One historian stated that Mifflin, "...performed his ammunition supply duties despite bursting enemy shells that swept away men stationed nearby." Such statements led to Mifflin's award through the issuance of General Orders No. 45 on December 31, 1864.[5]

The *U. S. S. Brooklyn* was decommissioned May 14, 1889 at the New York Navy Yard. The following year the vessel was struck from the Naval Register. E. J. Elder purchased the decommissioned two hundred thirty-three-foot boat March 25, 1891. The fate of the craft from that point forward is unknown.[6]

Sadly, no information related to the post-war life of James Mifflin is known to exist. Therefore, the date and location of his death, as well as his burial, are uncertain. The four hundred fifty-foot *U. S. S. Mifflin*, commissioned October 1944, was named in his honor and participated in the landings at Iwo Jima and Okinawa during World War 2. Able to handle a crew of eighty-seven officers and almost one thousand five hundred men, the *Mifflin* was sold to the West Waterway Lumber Company in 1975 for $128,000,000.[7]

CHAPTER TWENTY-TWO

Joachim Pease

One of the least-documented individuals to earn the Medal of Honor, Joachim Pease was reportedly born in 1842. Some uncertainty surrounds the location of his birth, but Long Island, New York is one proposed site. No additional information related to Pease exists until he became a member of the U. S. Navy. Records show that Joachim Pease enlisted for a three-year term beginning January 12, 1862.[1]

Pease listed his birthplace as Fogo Island; one historian has proposed that is Fogo Island, Cape Verde, located off the west coast of Africa. Other information related to Joachim Pease stated he was twenty years old, five feet, six and a half inches tall, with black hair and eyes and a "negro" complexion. In addition, Joachim Pease was a seaman aboard *U. S. S. Kearsarge* as the vessel neared Cherbourg, France on June 19, 1864. Pease served as a loader on Gun No. 2 that fateful day, and he was one of fifteen black sailors aboard the ship.[2]

Kearsarge was launched September 11, 1861 at the Portsmouth Navy Yard in Portsmouth, New Hampshire. Manned with a crew of one hundred sixty-two men, the ship was described as 214 feet long and contained an arsenal of two eleven-inch smooth bore Dahlgren cannons, one 30-pound Parrott rifle, and four 32-pound cannons. The vessel left Portsmouth February 5, 1862, headed to the Spanish coast to block Confederate raiders. On April 8, 1863, Captain John Winslow assumed command of *Kearsarge* as it remained in European waters.[3]

The *Alabama*, a Confederate sloop-of-war, had arrived in France in early June 1864 in order to release prisoners and take on coal. Eight days later, *Alabama* was located off the Cherbourg, France coast as *Kearsarge* engaged the vessel. *Alabama* was noted as "a close match" to the *Kearsarge*, as the Confederate vessel was 220 feet long and held an armament of one 68-pound cannon, a 110-pound rifled cannon, and six 32-pound cannons. Under the leadership of Captain Raphael Semmes, a crew of one hundred forty-eight men graced her decks. However, evidence indicates the *Alabama* was "reduced to a floating wreck" within an hour of the first shots from *Kearsarge*. An 1864 painting accredited to French artist Edouard Manet portrays *Alabama* "a scourge of Union shipping" as the vessel "sinks by her stern, clouds of smoke arising from a direct hit to her engines."[4]

According to witnesses, "a heaving turquoise, blue, and gray sea" relentlessly tossed surviving Confederate sailors who were "clinging to wreckage" as their ship sank stern first. A local pilot boat, as well as

Kearsarge, rescued Confederates from the waters. The battle proved a tragic end for a Confederate ship that had previously sunk sixty merchant ships and caused an estimated five million dollars in damage to the commerce of the United States.[5]

D. H. Sumner, Acting Master aboard *Kearsarge*, wrote of Pease, "But among those showing still higher qualifications I am pleased to name ...Robert Strahan, first captain of No. 1 gun; James H. Lee, sponger, and Joachim Pease... The conduct of the latter in battle fully sustained his reputation as one of the best men in the ship." Sumner added that Pease possessed "qualities higher than courage or fortitude" that solidified the superlative designation of Pease.[6]

Joachim Pease was additionally praised for his gallantry under fire. A divisional officer "highly recommended" the young man for the Medal of Honor. The citation for Pease's Medal of Honor states, in part, "The President of the United States, in the name of Congress, takes pleasure in presenting the Medal of Honor to Seaman Joachim Pease, United States Navy, for extraordinary heroism in action." Providing some insight into Pease's activities on board the *U. S. S. Kearsarge*, the citation explained that while the crew of ship destroyed the *Alabama*, Pease, "Acting as a loader...during this bitter engagement...exhibited marked coolness and good conduct and was highly recommended..."[7]

Joachim Pease became one of seventeen members of the *Kearsarge* crew to receive the Congressional Medal of Honor for bravery during the attack upon *CSS Alabama*. In addition to Pease, other Medal of Honor crewmen included Captain of the Top Robert Strahan, Captain of the Top John F. Bickford, Captain of the Forecastle James Haley, Quartermaster William Smith, Chief Quartermaster James Saunders, Quartermaster William Poole, and Paymaster Steward Michael Ahern. Other Medals earned went to Boatswain's Mate William S. Bond, Carpenter's Mate Mark G. Ham, Seaman George H. Harrison, Coxswain John Hayes, Seaman James H. Lee, and Seaman Charles Moore. The remaining Medal honorees included Boatswain's Mate Thomas Perry, Coxswain Charles A. Read and Seaman George E. Read.[8]

Joachim Pease, one of seven African American sailors to receive such a distinction during the American Civil War, was awarded the Medal of Honor on December 31, 1864. Unfortunately, he had evidently completed his term of enlistment by that time and did not receive the Medal. There is a positive note to the lack of presentation for Pease's Medal. Today, Joachim Pease's Medal of Honor can be viewed in the National Museum of the United States Navy in Washington, D. C. That facility is located on the grounds of the Washington Navy Yard and inside the former Breech Mechanism Shop of the Naval Gun Factory.[9]

As for the condition of Pease's Medal of Honor, it no longer has any type of suspension ribbon. However, holes for suspending the award are located near the top. The reverse side of Pease's Medal is engraved. The words of the engraved citation state, "Personal Valor: Joachim Pease: Colored Seaman: *U. S. S. Kearsarge*: Destruction of the *Alabama*: June 9, 1864."[10]

Upon his discharge from the Navy, Joachim Pease seems to have faded into oblivion. His post-war life, the date and location of his death, as well as the area in which he was buried are unknown statistics.[11]

CHAPTER TWENTY-THREE

Robert Pinn
(1843-1911)

Robert Alexander Pinn was born on a Perry Township, Ohio farm March 1, 1843, the sixth child in his family. His parents, William and Zilphia Broxton Pinn, lived on the farm and eventually had four additional children. William Pinn was a former slave from Fauquier County, Virginia; he had escaped slavery at the age of eighteen. Zilphia, a white resident of Stark County, was of English descent and a one-time resident of Mercer County, Pennsylvania.[1]

Robert Pinn apparently attended school and worked on the family's Ohio farm until he reached adulthood. He attempted to join the Federal army at the onset of the war, but his request was denied due to his race. He managed to join the 19th Ohio Infantry Regiment during the war's first year and served as a civilian worker for that unit.[2]

Though he held no military affiliation, Robert Pinn was able to move with the 19th Ohio Infantry Regiment as it marched south. He was at Shiloh in April 1862 and may have seen action there. Indications are that he saw action at other locations in the ensuing months despite not being enlisted.[3]

Robert Pinn was able to join the 5th United States Colored Troop, also known as the 127th Ohio Volunteer Infantry, in the months following the implementation of the Emancipation Proclamation. Pinn enlisted at Camp Delaware, Massillon, Ohio on September 5, 1863. Pinn, at the age of twenty, was recorded as standing six feet tall.[4]

Pinn later recalled his entry into the military, "I was very eager to become a soldier, in order to prove by my feeble efforts, the black man's rights to untrammeled manhood."[5]

Pinn's previous military experience, combat, and leadership abilities apparently gained quick recognition as he was promoted to the rank of sergeant on October

18, 1863, approximately one month after his enlistment. He received another promotion, to 1st sergeant, September 1, 1864.[6]

In May 1864, the 5th USCT or 127th Ohio moved to Fort Monroe, Virginia, as part of the "Colored Division" to join General Benjamin Butler in the advance toward Richmond. On June 15, 1864, Pinn was present at the assault and capture of Confederate entrenchments at Petersburg. General William Smith praised the African American soldiers in writing, "No troops ever did better fighting."[7]

Pinn and his fellow members of the 5th USCT were in the trenches surrounding Petersburg from the middle of June through mid-August 1864. In addition to occupying the trenches, the regiment-built fortifications. Subsequent actions for Robert Pinn included Deep Bottom, Virginia. There, many of the men in the 5th USCT served as Federal hospital orderlies.[8]

On September 29, 1864, 1st Sergeant Robert Pinn was at Chaffin's Farm, Virginia. During the battle, all the officers in his company were killed or wounded. Pinn took command of the unit and managed to lead them to victory and captured Fort Harrison. Later that day, the 5th USCT attacked Fort Gilmer, but strong Confederate counterattacks forced a Federal retreat.[9]

Robert Pinn was wounded three times during the action at New Market Heights and subsequent engagement at Fort Gilmer. His wounds necessitated hospital treatment, and he was confined to a medical facility in Portsmouth, Virginia. Sadly, one his wounds proved severe enough that Pinn permanently lost the use of his right arm.[10]

1st Sergeant Robert Pinn's actions at Fort Harrison soon earned recognition from General Benjamin Butler. On October 11, 1864, Butler wrote, "Robert Pinn, first sergeant, commanding Company I, wounded...will cause a special medal to be struck in honor of these gallant-colored soldiers."[11] Besides receiving the Butler Medal, an award paid for through the general's funds, another major honor awaited him.

Robert Pinn was awarded the Congressional Medal of Honor April 6, 1865. His bravery and heroism during the battle of New Market Heights or Chapin's/Chaffin's Farm was recognized with his citation. It read in part, "All...the company officers being killed or wounded, and [Pinn] led them gallantly and meritoriously through the day."[12]

When the war concluded later that month, Pinn's regiment primarily served as garrison troops at Goldsboro, North Carolina. That assignment ended with similar duties in Newbern and Carolina City, North Carolina. Some sources indicate Robert Pinn was mustered out of service in Carolina City, North Carolina September 20, 1865. However, additional information states that the 5th USCT was ordered to Columbus, Ohio in September 1865 and was mustered out of service to the United States on October 5, 1865.[13]

Returning to his hometown, Pinn married Mahoning County resident Emily Manzilla. The couple eventually had one daughter, Gracie Pinn Brooks. Another activity for Pinn took place in 1866. That year, "he submitted an autobiographical essay to a left-handed penmanship competition organized by a newspaper editor to promote the cause of disabled veterans." [14]

In his post war years, Robert Pinn secured employment as a teamster and a contractor. He left Massillon to attend Oberlin College and briefly taught school in both Cairo, Illinois and Newberry, South Carolina. A tenure as a claim agent for the U. S. Prison Bureau occupied additional time in his life. Pinn was a Mason and was a member and eventual commander of the Hart Post 134 of the Grand Army of the Republic, the first African American to hold that position in the post. Additionally, Robert Pinn served as a delegate to the 1891 Ohio Republican Convention that nominated William McKinley for governor of Ohio.[15]

Robert Pinn was admitted to the Ohio bar in 1879. His abilities as an attorney were emphasized in a tribute from the Stark County Bar Association at the time of Robert Pinn's death. It was stated that Pinn held "more than ordinary ability in the examination of witnesses and the trial of causes. He was a fluent and forceful speaker without bombast or flourish."[16]

At the age of sixty-seven, Robert Pinn passed away January 1, 1911 in his Massillon, Ohio home. He was interred in the Brooks family plot, Section 1, Lot 47, and Grave 18737 of the Massillon Cemetery.[17]

An Ohio historical marker is dedicated to Robert Pinn. It can be found on Erie Street South in Massillon. The postal address close to the marker's location is 1827 Eric St. S. Massillon, Ohio, 44646.[18]

Almost a century after his heroic actions that earned him the Medal of Honor, Robert Alexander Pinn was memorialized in another manner. The National Guard Armory in Stow, Ohio was completed in 1973 and named in honor of Pinn.[19]

Twenty-five years later, in 1998, The University of Akron renamed its shooting facility the Robert A. Pinn Shooting Range. The university's rifle team and ROTC members utilize the facility that is regarded as one of the best in the state.[20]

CHAPTER TWENTY-FOUR

Edward Ratcliff
(1835-1915)

Walnut trees towered above a two-story James City County, Virginia farmhouse on February 8, 1835. Nearby, a small shack served as the birthplace of Edward Ratcliff. The infant was the child of a slave named Hannah and a white father.[1]

The plantation where Edward Ratcliff was born had a long and interesting history. In 1657, the original two hundred acres of the farm were granted to John Hankins, an Englishman. John's son, Charles, increased the size of the farm to three-hundred seventy acres, and he owned ten slaves. Charles and his wife, Druisilla, eventually had four children; their youngest was a son named Nathaniel. As the number of slaves increased under Nathaniel's tenure, so did the offspring of Nathaniel and Betsy, his bride.[2]

One of Nathaniel and Betsy Hankins's children was named Alexander. In time, Alexander inherited the farm of more than four hundred acres and the slaves who lived there. One of the slaves was Edward Ratcliff, a two-year-old at the time. By 1850, Alexander Hankins owned twenty-two slaves, including ten adults. At that time, Edward Ratcliff was approximately fifteen years of age.[3]

By 1854, Alexander Hankins managed to increase his land holdings to almost seven hundred acres. To accomplish that task, Hankins had to mortgage eight of his slaves. One of those was a young lady named Grace. Edward Ratcliff was in love with Grace. Four years later, on July 9, 1858, Edward Ratcliff and Grace were married in a ceremony that Scott Hankins, one of Alexander's sons, performed.[4]

On March 24, 1861, weeks before Confederate forces fired upon Fort Sumter, South Carolina, Grace and Edward Ratcliff had a daughter who they named Hannah.[5]

Two months later, in May 1861, Federal General Benjamin Butler, the commander of the Department of Virginia, stated that runaway slaves were to be considered contraband of war. As such, they were "subject to seizure by the military." In that situation, the slaves would not be returned to their owners. The nearby Federal fort in Hampton became affectionately known among African Americans as Fort Freedom.[6]

Ratcliff family historian Stephanie Heinatz wrote, "Edward Ratcliff had a family to care for. He stayed on the Hankins farm with Grace and Hannah." The Emancipation Proclamation proposed freedom for Southern slaves. When black men were later encouraged to serve in the U. S. military, Edward Ratcliff felt a stronger obligation to fight.[7]

At a 2011 Black History Month program featuring a presentation on Edward Ratcliff, a guest speaker said, "...he worked as a slave...from sun-up to sun-down, working long hours, not being able to come and go as you please." It was also stated that Ratcliff left the farm in the dead of winter to fight for the freedom of his family, others, and himself, and that, in doing so, he ended his "laboring in the fields of a several-hundred-acre plantation in James City County."[8]

A Ratcliff family historian, noting the surname has been changed to Radcliff in the ensuing decades, explains the city of Yorktown was taken from the Confederates, setting the stage for Ratcliff's entry into military service. The historian wrote, "Slaves from across the region bravely left their homes, flocking to Union army camps. They traded their life of bondage for the unknowns of life as a refugee...looked to the military for food, work and protection."[9]

Edward Ratcliff, under that scenario, entered the United States Army at Yorktown, Virginia January 1, 1864. His enlistment papers note that he was twenty-nine at the time of his three-year enlistment. Ratcliff then became a member of the 38th U. S. Colored Troops. Originally in Company I, Ratcliff was eventually transferred to Company C and promoted to the rank of 1st Sergeant. His regiment was assigned to the 3rd Division, 18th Corps, Army of the James. That division was exclusively comprised of black soldiers and white officers.[10]

Edward Ratcliff's first taste of combat was in June 1864 at Petersburg. His division was able to capture Confederate artillery pieces before being forced from the area. The men in blue then manned the trenches surrounding Petersburg and began a siege of the town.[11]

Edward Ratcliff and the men of the 3rd Division received their marching orders on September 27, 1864. They were to prepare three days' rations and procure a blanket and sixty rounds of ammunition. Travelling north along the James River, the troops established camp at Chaffin's Farm, where the "first of several lines of the city's fortifications" were located.[12]

On the foggy morning of September 29, 1864, 1st Sergeant Edward Ratcliff made his way through a swampy region of the James River south of Richmond, Virginia, the Confederate capital city. General Benjamin Butler, a Federal general who did not doubt the ability of African American soldiers in combat, ordered the men of the 38th U. S. C. T. to advance against the Confederate fortifications at Chaffin's Farm and New Market Heights. However, Butler's orders also included the stipulation that Ratcliff and his fellow regimental members were to only use their bayonets. No guns were to be fired.[13]

Before issuing his order to use only bayonets in the shoulder-to-shoulder march, Butler had arrived at 4:30 a.m. and found, "the colored division...occupying a plain which shelved towards the river...not observed by the enemy...I told them they must take it at all hazards."[14]

The rationale behind Butler's orders was that the fog would likely negate clear vision and possibly cause the advancing Federals to shoot one another. As the Confederates began blasting the Federal ranks, Ratcliff's commanding officer, a captain, was killed. That situation left 1st Sergeant Ratcliff in command.[15]

Ratcliff ordered his troops forward, and the soldiers raised their muskets above their heads as they marched through the deep swamp. The situation in which the Federal soldiers found themselves was difficult, to say the least. One participant noted, "The fog enwrapped [us] like a mantle of death." Another stated that the advance was made through "a hail of bullets."[16]

In response to 1st Sergeant Edward Ratcliff's actions at Fort Harrison, General Benjamin Butler made an October 11, 1864 statement regarding a major recognition. General Butler exclaimed, "First Sergt. Edward Ratcliff...thrown into command of his company by the death of the officer commanding, was the first enlisted man in the enemy's works, leading his company with great gallantry, for which he has a medal."[17] As such, Ratcliff became a recipient of the Butler Medal, an award General Butler created and funded.

In addition to the Butler Medal, an additional accolade came Ratcliff's way in the form of a military advancement. On December 24, 1864, Edward Ratcliff was promoted to the rank of sergeant-major. The promotion was reportedly made for his gallantry exhibited during the action at Fort Harrison.[18]

1st Sergeant Edward Ratcliff was awarded the Medal of Honor, for "his heroism and selfless devotion to duty" on April 6, 1865. A portion of Edward Ratcliff's Medal of Honor citation stated of him, "Commanded and gallantly led his company after the commanding officer had been killed, was the first enter the enemy's works." Sergeant-major Edward Ratcliff was mustered out of service at Indianola, Texas January 25, 1867.[19]

When his military career came to an end, Edward Ratcliff returned to York County and his family. By the age of thirty-two he was suffering from rheumatism. He had reportedly caught a severe cold while in Texas, and the effects of that had remained. Despite his physical ailments, Edward Ratcliff and his wife were able to increase the size of their family. In 1869, Lucie, their second child, was born. Two years later, Bennett, their first son, arrived. Annie, Samuel, Charles, and U. S. Grant, Edward and Grace's fourth through seventh children, were born in 1874, 1876, 1878, and 1881, respectfully.[20]

The family worshipped at St. John's Baptist Church. Regarding the scheduled services, "Sunday school was in the morning...morning worship once a month, on the third Sunday."[21]

As the 1880s progressed, Ratcliff's health seriously declined. He made an unsuccessful request for a pension when his 1890 request was denied. A second pension plea was also ignored. Edward Ratcliff's family physician filed an affidavit in 1892 and used the opportunity to emphasize the diagnosis of rheumatism and failing eyesight as disabilities that hampered the life of the Medal of Honor recipient. The physician's intervention evidently aided Ratcliff's cause, as the government agreed in 1895 to begin paying Ratcliff a pension of $6 per month.[22]

Yet another malady affected Edward Ratcliff. An 1894 physical examination showed that his pulse stood at a normal rate of 88, his weight was 155 pounds, and the one-time soldier was capable of rising and stooping without difficulty. However, within a year, Ratcliff had lost most of his teeth due to scurvy. In the ensuing years, weight loss became an issue for him. His summer 1895 weight was 141. Six years later, Edward Ratcliff weighed 133 pounds. Those issues, along with his ever-increasing loss of vision, enabled Ratcliff to begin receiving an increased pension of $12 per month.[23]

Edward Ratcliff lost Grace in the midst of these health issues. He remarried at the age of seventy-seven, and his pension was eventually increased to $30 per month. However, Ratcliff made a final visit to his doctor in late January 1915. The diagnosis confirmed Edward Ratcliff had contracted tuberculosis. On March 10, 1915, Edward Ratcliff passed away at the age of 80.[24]

Edward Ratcliff's place of burial was in Lackey, Virginia, at a location referred to as Kiskiak, the Native American word for an area village. Local residents called the site "the reservation" due to the large concentration of American Indians and freed slaves. Sadly, three years after Ratcliff's death, the cemetery and surrounding land were deeded to the U. S. government, and a military base, known today as Yorktown Naval Weapons Station, was established. The area became off limits to the public. The wooden grave markers, such as the one used to mark Ratcliff's grave, rotted. The church building fell into disrepair.[25] Efforts of local historians such as Wes Wilson and Don Morfe, as well as descendants of Edward Ratcliff, enabled the erection of a 295-pound marker in the general area of long-lost grave of the Medal of Honoree. The short inscription says, "Medal of Honor. Sergeant Major, Company C, 38th United States Colored Troops. February 8, 1835 to March 10, 1915."[26]

CHAPTER TWENTY-FIVE

Andrew Jackson Smith
(1843-1932)

Andrew Jackson Smith was born a slave September 3, 1843 in Grand Rivers, Kentucky. His mother was a slave named Susan; his father was Elijah Smith, a slave owner. Little information exists in relation to Smith's early years aside from the fact that at age ten, Andrew Jackson Smith was given the task of operating a ferry that moved people and supplies across the Cumberland River. Andy, as young Smith was known, served as a boatman for approximately eight years.[1]

Elijah Smith, Andy's slave owning father, joined the Army of the Confederate States of America soon after the War Between the States began. Within a year, Elijah Smith returned home briefly. At the age of nineteen, Andrew Jackson Smith was scheduled to accompany Elijah Smith as the latter returned to the service of the Confederacy. It was an intermittent practice of the time for wealthy slave owners to take at least one slave while serving. When Andrew Jackson Smith became aware of Elijah Smith's intentions, Smith and another slave, Alfred "Alf" Bissell, determined it would be beneficial for them to run away.[2]

Smith and Bissell traveled an estimated twenty-five miles in freezing and rainy weather, to Smithland, Kentucky in order to contact the 41st Illinois Infantry Regiment, a unit serving the United States. Smithland, located at the convergence of the Cumberland and Ohio Rivers, was an outpost for the United States, a bit of information Andy Smith had learned while honing his skills on the river. The determination of the two runaways was made evident in the fact that their clothing had frozen to their bodies. Major John Warner, an officer in the 41st Illinois, employed Andrew Jackson Smith as his servant. Alfred Bissell secured a similar position with Colonel Isaac Campbell Pugh, the commander of the 41st Illinois. A major function Smith was to perform in the designation as Major Warner's servant was to return

Warner's possessions to Clinton, Illinois, Warner's home, should the major die.[3]

With a letter, Major Warner notified his family about the arrangement with Andy. Little time existed for gaining familiarity with one another as the 41st Illinois moved toward Fort Henry, Tennessee to engage the Confederates. The battle was quick and decisive; the fort fell. In turn, the 41st Illinois moved to Fort Donelson where stubborn Confederate resistance led to approximately two hundred regimental casualties.[4]

Having been at Fort Donelson, the 41st Illinois Infantry Regiment moved to the vicinity of Pittsburg Landing, Tennessee in March 1862. The following month, that location, situated near Shiloh Church, became the sight of a major battle. In that engagement, nineteen-year-old Andrew Jackson Smith was able to supply Major Warner with fresh horses, required when the officer had two of the animals shot from under him.[5]

In the course of the two days of action at Shiloh, Andrew Jackson Smith endured incidents that could have easily been fatal. An Illinois State University history professor noted in a postwar account that the initial contact between Smith and a bullet proved minor in writing, "The first one knocked him down, but he shook it off." Subsequently, a spent lead slug struck Smith's left temple and made a shallow entry into his skin. Moving along Smith's head, the projectile advanced to the middle of his forehead where it became lodged. Fortunately, a regimental surgeon was able to remove the ball, and a small permanent scar on Andrew Jackson Smith's head was the only enduring evidence.[6]

Although Andrew Jackson Smith was able to escape serious injury at Shiloh, a succeeding ailment proved critical to his health and military service. An intestinal disorder necessitated Smith's temporary leave from military service. In turn, he proceeded to his home in Clinton, Illinois in order to recover. The strong relationship that evidently existed between Andrew Jackson Smith and Major Warner is emphasized in a quote from a modern historian who penned, "Smith's wound wasn't much of a problem, but Warner wanted to take Smith to Clinton where he would be safe and protected by Warner's family." Having been promoted to the rank of colonel, Warner accompanied Andy Smith to Clinton, Illinois in November 1862.[7]

While recovering in Clinton, Andrew Jackson Smith was made aware of the Emancipation Proclamation. As soon as he was able to make the journey, Smith, using funds Major Warner provided, made his way to Boston, Massachusetts in order to join the 54th Massachusetts. Apparently having acquired enough men to fill its ranks, the 54th Massachusetts did not enlist Smith. Not to be deterred in his quest to become a member of the United States Army, Smith joined the 55th Massachusetts May 16, 1863. In the following months, Smith was promoted to the rank of corporal.[8]

As a member of Company B in the 55th Massachusetts, Corporal Andrew Jackson Smith and his fellow regimental members joined the 54th Massachusetts soon after the latter unit fought in the famed July 1863 assault against Battery Wagner. The two regiments fought five military engagements together in the following months. In addition to the combat in which the 54th and 55th Massachusetts Regiments endured, they also successfully strived to receive pay equal to that of white soldiers. Noting Smith's character, one historian stated, "...in order to receive his pay, a black soldier was required to nod his head [to the affirmative] when asked if he was free in 1861." Smith refused to lie, although his honesty would negate his receipt of additional pay.[9]

By late 1864, Andrew Jackson Smith was a member of the 1,040-man 2nd Infantry Brigade, Colored, under the command of Colonel Gallant Hartwell. The 54th and 55th Massachusetts Infantry Regiments joined the 102nd, 26th, and 34th USCT to form the infantry portions of the brigade. Three artillery brigades and three sailor, marine, and naval battalions rounded out the unit.[10]

On November 30, 1864, Corporal Andrew Jackson Smith and the men of the 54th and 55th Massachusetts Infantry Regiments combined their efforts in an engagement at Honey Hill, South Carolina. The location was situated "at the headwaters of the Broad River along the Charleston and Savannah Railroad." The engagement was the first at the railroad junction. As the two Massachusetts regiments made their way through a narrow gorge that crossed a swamp situated in front of the elevated Confederate position, heavy Confederate fire riddled their ranks.[11]

The Confederate post at Honey Hill was considered weaker on the flanks than at the center. The artillery redoubt that Smith and the additional members of the 55th Massachusetts faced was recalled as "an open earthwork with embrasures for four guns and extended two hundred feet on each side of the Grahamville Road. The terrain immediately in front of the artillery redoubt was comparatively open. At 150 yards to the front, the shallow, sluggish Euhaw Creek, two feet deep and twenty yards wide, opened up into a marsh..."[12]

In the ensuing action, Corporal Andrew Jackson Smith joined his fellow regiment members in a series of three charges. Smith also witnessed the death of the regiment's color-bearer, Sergeant Robert King, who according to one historian, was the victim of "canister shot, lead or steel balls packed in sawdust and fired, shotgun like, from cannons." Smith managed to not only carry the U. S. flag, but he also grasped the regimental flag when Sergeant King fell. Smith, known among fellow soldiers as Andy, grabbed Old Glory and waved the colors over his head. The twenty-one-year-old Smith then led his compatriots toward the Confederate position.[13]

It was written about Andrew Jackson Smith that he "continued to expose himself to enemy fire by carrying the colors throughout the battle. Through his actions, the Regimental Colors of the 55th Infantry Regiment were not lost to the enemy." Additionally, the author of that statement said Smith's "valor in the face of deadly enemy fire is in keeping with the highest traditions of military service, and reflects great credit upon him, the 55th Regiment, and the United States Army." Those accomplishments and the worthiness of praises are made more profound when noting that half of the officers and a third of the enlisted men of the 55th Massachusetts were killed or wounded during the Battle of Honey Hill.[14]

Colonel Alfred Hartwell of the 55th Massachusetts wrote, "The leading brigade had been driven back...I was knocked out...Captain Crane, was killed...During the furious fight...Andrew Jackson Smith...would retrieve and save both the State and Federal flags."[15]

The tenacity of the Battle of Honey Hill is reflected in the losses the conflicting armies suffered. Seven hundred forty-six Federals were reported as casualties. Although unrecorded, Confederate casualties were estimated at one hundred. That estimate was reinforced in a Savannah newspaper that stated, "Our loss was between 80 and 100 killed and wounded."[16]

In the aftermath of the battle at Honey Hill, South Carolina, Andrew Jackson Smith was recognized for his heroism. Smith was promoted to the rank of color sergeant. Smith was discharged at Mt. Pleasant, South Carolina August 29, 1865.[17] Other acknowledgements of Smith's efforts at Honey Hill would inspire efforts across the century and a half that lay ahead.

The regimental commander of the 55th Massachusetts had suffered a severe wound during the early stages of the battle at Honey Hill. That wound and the following period of recovery delayed the timely filing of the official report on the battle. Other officers were wounded as well, and the battle aspects that could have quickly led to "the cherished Medal of Honor for Andy's bravery at Honey Hill" was, unfortunately, "never fully documented, and Andy's heroics could not be certified." This delay, according to one historian, may have created the inability of Smith to receive the ultimate recognition for which many individuals felt he was due.[18]

Additional accolades for Andrew Jackson Smith were offered in the aftermath of the battle at Honey Hill. A surgeon who served with Smith nominated the Kentucky-born soldier for the Medal of Honor. The physician's actions took place in 1916, decades after the end of the war. By that time, Smith was seventy-three years old. According to an authority on Smith's life, "The Army rejected the nomination, citing lack of evidence." U. S. Senator Dick Durbin, an Illinois Democrat, later noted that racism was a likely factor in the denunciation. One historian added that the prejudice present at the time of the rejection to present Smith with the Medal of Honor also denied African Americans the ability to serve as combat troops in World War I.[19]

A letter from Vespasian Warner, Major Warner's son, added support to the plea for Smith to be awarded the Medal of Honor. The letter stated, "Mr. Andy Smith of Grand River, Kentucky, having asked me to write you what I remember in relation to a wound he received at the battle of Shiloh...after my father's regiment became engaged the horse on which he was mounted was wounded and my father was dismounted and turning found Andy standing close to him and giving the wounded horse to Andy, told him to take it to the rear and stay there. A short time afterwards a horse from which some Confederate had been shot, galloped out between the lines and my father rushed out, caught and mounted him. Soon afterward this second horse was wounded and my father again dismounted and turning, found Andy standing close to him again and handing the second horse to Andy, told him to take it back and keep out of danger, and just then Andy received a gunshot wound in the head from the enemy. The above is all I remember of the matter. Andy was certainly...brave and loyal..."[20]

After his discharge, the frugal Andy Smith settled in Clinton, Illinois for a short time. He returned to Kentucky and used his mustering out pay to buy land. Having been aware of the failed efforts to award him with the Medal of Honor, Smith continued to buy and sell land in his native state of Kentucky. His landholdings eventually approached one thousand acres.[21]

In relation to his personal life, Smith was recorded as being twenty-six during the 1870 census. Living in Lyon, Kentucky at the time, he and his twenty-seven-year-old wife, Mandy, had a daughter, Caruth. The 1910 census noted that Smith was a sixty-seven-year-old widower.[22]

Eighty-eight-year-old Andrew Jackson Smith passed away in Livingston County, Kentucky March 4, 1932. He was buried in Mount Pleasant Cemetery, Lyon County, near Grand Rivers, Kentucky.[23]

Between the Rivers Inc., an organization from the vicinity where Andy Smith spent many years of his life, managed to earn Smith the recognition its members felt he deserved. A Kentucky Historical Society marker was placed in the Land Between the Lakes in order to memorialize Smith. More specifically, the metal olive-green tablet rests at the base of the hill where Andrew Jackson Smith's grave is located. Oak and cedar trees shade the grave that is marked with a Medal of Honor tombstone which Between the Rivers, Inc. assisted in placing.[24]

Indianapolis resident Andrew Smith Bowman, grandson of Andrew Jackson Smith, struggled for years to gain additional recognition of Smith's actions at Honey Hill. U. S. Senator Dick Durbin and U. S. Representative Tom Ewing of Illinois joined Bowman. On January 16, 2001, one hundred thirty-seven years after the Honey Hill engagement, President Bill Clinton presented the long overdue Medal of Honor to descendants of Andrew Jackson Smith.[25]

The official citation for Andrew Jackson Smith's Medal of Honor stated, "For conspicuous gallantry and intrepidity at the risk of his life above and beyond the call of duty: Corporal Andrew Jackson Smith, of Clinton, Illinois, a member of the 55th Massachusetts Voluntary Infantry, distinguished himself on 30 November 1864 by saving his regimental colors, after the color bearer was killed during a bloody charged the Battle of Honey Hill, South Carolina. In the late afternoon, as the 55th Regiment pursued enemy skirmishers and conducted a running fight, they ran into a swampy area backed by a rise where the Confederate Army awaited. The surrounding woods and thick underbrush impeded infantry movement and artillery support...As the Confederates repelled other units, the 55th and 54th regiments continued to move into flanking positions. Forced into a narrow gorge crossing a swamp in the face of the enemy positions, the 55th's Color-Sergeant was killed by an exploding shell, and Corporal Smith took the Regimental Colors from his hand and carried them through heavy grape and canister.[26]

As such, Andrew Jackson Smith's heroic actions exhibited during the Battle of Honey Hill were finally recognized with the long-desired and fitting results.

CHAPTER TWENTY-SIX

Charles Veale (Veal) (1838-1872)

Little information exists in relation to the early years in the life of Charles Veale. He was born in Portsmouth, Virginia in 1838, but the exact month and day are unknown. There is also discrepancy in his surname as it was sometimes spelled Veal.[1]

From records of his indoctrination, the 25-year-old Veale indicated his profession as a fireman at the time of his July 28, 1863 enlistment. Joining the military in Baltimore, Veale was noted as standing approximately five feet and three inches tall. Private Charles Veale served in Company D of the 4th United States Colored Infantry, and he was promoted to the rank of corporal November 12, 1863.[2]

On September 29, 1864, Charles Veale joined his fellow regiment members as they moved against the Confederates positioned at Chaffin's Farm, or New Market Heights, a position located near Richmond, Virginia. Veale witnessed two of his fellow soldiers fall as each held a flag. As has been noted, "...flags allowed soldiers to know the position of their units, and which direction they should be moving to keep up with it. Flag bearers carried them at enormous risk to their lives."[3]

Sergeant Alfred Hilton was situated near Veale as they advanced toward the Confederates. Hilton was bearing two flags when a serious wound forced him to dispose of his colors. Sergeant Christian Fleetwood secured the National colors; Veale managed to grab the blue regimental flag. Both banners were rescued before hitting the ground. The two men managed to continue their advance against the Confederate position while also hoisting their respective flag and motivating the troops. Approximately six months later, Veale received the Medal of Honor for his heroism at Chaffin's Farm.[4]

The primary words of Veale's Medal of Honor citation misspelled his surname as Veal. The citation stated in part, "Seized the national colors, after two color bearers had been shot down close to the enemy's works and bore them through the remainder of the battle."[5]

In an October 11, 1864 order, General Benjamin Butler had offered additional praise to Charles Veale by adding, "He has a medal for gallantry, and will have the warrant of color-sergeant." The medal to which Butler referred was the Butler Medal, one which General Butler funded and presented. Butler's admiration of Veale's actions led to Butler promoting Veale to the rank of sergeant; the rank became official November 12, 1864. Also, General Butler pinned the Medal of Honor of Veale's chest in a presentation held April 6, 1865.[6]

Recalling Veale's actions of September 29, 1864, a soldier who served with Veale stated, "I have never been able to understand how Veal [sic] and I lived under such a hail of bullets unless it was because we were both such little fellows. I think I weighed…125 pounds…Veal… the same. We did not get a scratch." Those statements are more eye-opening when one becomes aware that about one hundred eighty men from the 4th USCT were casualties that day.[7]

Veale's military activities for the duration of the war included action at Fair Oaks in October 1864, as well as Fort Fisher in the ensuing months. He was reportedly wounded at Fort Fisher. His regiment participated in engagements at Sugar Loaf Hill, Fort Anderson, Wilmington, and the Carolinas. The unit was mustered out of service May 4, 1866, having lost a total of two hundred ninety-two men during its tenure of military service.[8] Little is known about Veale's post-war activities. Sadly, Charles Veale passed away July 27, 1872 in Hampton, Virginia. Due to the uncertainty of his birthday, he was either thirty-three or thirty-four at the time of his death. Veale was buried in the Hampton National Cemetery.[9]

Endnotes

Introduction
1. "United States Colored Troops: Civil War Memorial Monument." https://www.hmdb.org/marker.asp?marker=56476.
2. Ibid; Percoco, Jim. "The United States Colored Troops." https://civilwar.org/learn/ articles/united-states-colored-troops.
3. Kammen, Carol. "Guest Essay: Black Troops, White Civil War Units" http://newyorkhistoryblog.org/2012/01/23/guest-essay-black-troops-white- civil-war-units; "Black Troops in Union Blue." http://www.crf-usa.org/black-history-month/black-troops-in-blue;" "Colored Troops in the American Civil War." https://americancivilwar.com/colored/colored_troops.html.
4. "United States Colored Troops: Civil War Memorial Monument." https://www.hmdb.org; Kammen, Carol.
5. Freeman, Elise; Wynell Burroughs Schamel, and Jean West. "The Fight for Equal Rights: A Recruiting Poster for Black Soldiers in the Civil War." Social Education 56, 2 (February 1992. 118; "History of the Colored Troops in the American Civil War." https://americancivilwar.com/colored/histofcoloredtroops.html; "Stories." https://www.nps.gov/afam/learn/historyculture/stories.htm.
6. Feber, Eric. "Medal of Honor winners to be recognized." The Virginian-Pilot. November 10, 2006. http://pilotonline.com/news/local/article_301af75e-d911-5d97-a92b-2e00602689-e8.html.
7. Percoco; "Colored Troops in the American Civil War."
8. Freeman, Elise... "The Fight for Equal Rights."
9. "Black Troops in Union Blue." http://www.crf-usa.org.
10. Ibid; "History of the Colored Troops in the American Civil War;" "African-American Soldiers During the Civil War." http://www.loc.gov/teachers/classroom-Materials/ presentation-sandactivities/presentations/timeline/civilwar/aasoldrs; "African Americans in the Armed Forces Timeline." https://www.civilwar.org/learn/articles/african- americans-armed-forces-timeline.
11. "On the Battlefield." https://www.nps.gov/parkhistory/online_books/ civil_war_series/2/sec18.htm.
12. Wertz, Frederick. "For love of Old Glory: Civil War Medals of Honor." https://blog.findmy-past.com/community/frederick_wertz.

13. Gilkes, Paul. "Joachim Pease Medal of Honor from Civil War on public display in Washington,D.C." https://www.coinworld.com/news/us-coins/2017/10/joachim-pease-congressional-medal-of-honor.all.htm.
14. Ibid.
15. Ibid.

Chapter 1—Aaron Anderson
1. "Rhumb Lines." Navy Office of Information. January 14, 2009; Aaron Anderson. https://civilwarpvmhs.weebly.com/aaron-anderson.html.
2. "Sanderson, Aaron." http://www.homeofhearoes.com/moh/citations_1862_cwq/ sanderson.html; "Anderson, Aaron—Medal of Honor." http://historymugs.us/product/ aaron-anderson-medal-of-honor/.
3. *"Wyandank."* http://www.navsource.org/archives/09/86/86063.htm.
4. *Official Records of the Union and Confederate navies in the War of the Rebellion.* Washington, D.C.: Government Printing Office, 1897. Referred to hereafter as O.R.
5. "Mattox Creek." https://www.revolvy.com/main/index.php?s=Mattox+Creek &item_type=topic.
6. Ibid; Hedelt, Rob. "Upcoming Stratford Hall program to detail heroics of medal-winning African American sailor." *The Free Lance-Star.* February 8, 2018.
7. Hedelt; "7 Historical Civil War Figures Who Don't Have a Statue, But Deserve One." HuffPost Partner Studio. January 11, 2017.
8. Hedelt; "Black History Month Highlight: Aaron Anderson." http://civilwarnavy150.blog spotcom/ 2011/02/black-history-month-highlight-aaron.html.
9. Ibid; Who Were These Heroes?" Negro History Bulletin. Vol. 23, No. 3, December 1959. p. 50.
10. Hedelt; "Return of a Death in the City of Philadelphia—1886," no. 1139. Philadelphia Municipal Archives.
11. "Return of a Death…1886;" "Aaron Anderson…Honor;" "Sanderson, Aaron."

Chapter 2----Bruce Anderson
1. "PVT Bruce Anderson." https://www.findagrave.com/memorial/5747861/bruce-anderson; Steelman, Ben. "Black soldier persevered for Medal of Honor." Star News Online. http://www.stamewsonline.com/news/20150228/black-soldier-persevered-for-medal-of-honor; "June 19—Happy Birthday Bruce Anderson." The Amsterdam, NY Blog; "Bruce Anderson, War Hero." https://www.famousbirthdays.com/people/bruce-anderson.html.

2. "Bruce...Hero;" Steelman; "June...Anderson;" Moss, Juanita Patience. *The Forgotten Black Soldiers in White Regiments During the Civil War.* Westminster, Maryland: Heritage Books. 2008; Cannon, Helen. "Medal of Honor for Fort Fisher Action." http://nccivilwarcenter.org/medal-honor-fort-fisher-action; "Photo of Grave site of MOH Recipient Bruce Anderson." http://www.homeofheroes.com/gravesites/states/pages_af/ Anderson.bruce_ny.html; "African-American private was a Civil War hero." http://www.wral.com/african-american-private-was-a-civil-war-hero/14368826/.
3. Steelman; "June...Anderson;" Phisterer, Frederick. *New York in the War of the Rebellion.* Albany: J. B. Lyon Company. 1912.
4. "Fort Fisher, Second Battle of Fort Fisher." https://www.civilwar.org/learn/civil-war/battles/fort-fisher; "Fort Fisher State Historic Site." http://www.nchistoricsites. org/fisher/.
5. Landsman, Danie. "The Fall of Fort Fisher." https://www.civilwar.org/learn/articles/fall-fort-fisher; "Fort Fisher State Historic Site."
6. "June 19...Anderson;" *The Union army: a history of military affairs in the loyal states, 1861-65—records of the regiments in the Union army—cyclopedia of battles---memoirs of commanders and soldiers.* Vol. II. Madison, WI. Federal Publishing Company. 1908.
7. *The Union army... commanders and soldiers.*
8. "June 19...Anderson."
9. Chaitin, Peter M., ed. *The Coastal War: Chesapeake to Rio Grande.* Alexandria, Va: Time-Life Books. 1984.
10. Landsman, "The Fall of Fort Fisher;" "Fort Fisher...Site;" OR, 16, 154.
11. Gragg, Rod. *Confederate Goliath: The Battle of Fort Fisher.* Baton Rouge: Louisiana State University Press. 1994, 121, 131.
12. Landsman, "The Fall of Fort Fisher."
13. Ibid; Gragg, 135.
14. Steelman; "June 19...Anderson;" "African-American private was a Civil War hero;" Cudmore, Bob. "Storming Fort Fisher during the Civil War." https://dailygazette.com/article/2014/09/13/storming-fort-fisher-during-civil-war.
15. Cudmore.
16. Steelman; "African-American private was a Civil War hero;" Reagen, James E. "African Americans fought at Fort Fisher." The Daily News. February 11, 2016. http://www. thedailynewsonline.com/blogs/african-americans-fought-at-fort-Fisher-20160211; Reagen, James E. "Our Forgotten Heroes of Fort Fisher." The Daily News. February 18, 2016. http://www.ogd.com/blogs/our-forgotten-heroes-of-fort-fisher-20160218.

17. Phisterer, Frederick. *New York...*
18. Gragg, 192.
19. Cudmore.
20. Steelman.
21. Cudmore; Reagen, James E. "Our Forgotten Heroes of Fort Fisher."
22. Steelman; "PVT...Anderson;" Cannon, "Medal of Honor..."
23. Steelman.
24. Ibid; "PVT...Anderson;" "Photo of grave site...Anderson;" "Bruce...hero;" Gerth, Adrian. "The Gibraltar of the South." https://capefearlivingmagazine.com/the-gibraltar-of-the-south.
25. Reagen, "Our Forgotten...Fisher."
26. Steelman; Cannon, "Medal of Honor...;" "Bruce...hero;" Moss, Juanita Patience. *The Forgotten Black Soldiers in White Regiments During the Civil War.* Westminster, Maryland: Heritage Books. 2008. 14.

Chapter 3--- William Barnes
1. "William H. Barnes." http://msa.maryland.gov/megafile/msa/speccol/sc3500 /sc3520/004600/004684/html/04684bio.html; Todd, Tom. "SGT William H Barnes." https://www.findagrave.com/memorial/18172/william-h-barnes; Ralston, Gary. "Sgt. William H. Barnes—MOH." http://indianolatx.com/BarnesWH.html.
2. Ibid; William H. Barnes---Compiled service record from http://www.calhouncountyhc.org/Marker_BarnesWH.pdf .
3. "38th Regiment, United States Colored Infantry." https://web.archive.org/web/ 20080410173040/www.itd.nps.gov/cwss/regiments.cfm; "38th United States Colored Troops." http://civilwarintheeast.com/us-regiments-batteries/us-Coloredtroops/ 38th- united-states-colored-troops; Civil War Soldiers and Sailors System. National Park Service. Archived from the original http://www.itd.nps.gov/cwss/regiments.cfm.
4. "38th United States Colored Troops."
5. "Medal of Honor: Heroes of the Battle of Chaffin's Farm." https://www.cem.va.gov/ CEM/pdf/Medal_of_Honor_Narratives_Heroes_Chapins_Farm.pdf.
6. Ralston; Berg, Gordon. "Battle of New Market Heights: USCT Soldiers Proved Their Heroism." America's Civil War. March 2006.
7. Berg.
8. Ralston.
9. Berg.
10. "Medal of Honor: Heroes of the Battle of Chaffin's Farm."
11. Berg.
12. "William H. Barnes." http://msa.maryland.gov/megafile/msa/speccol/sc3500/ sc3520/004600/004684/html/04684bio.html; "Civil

War Medal of Honor recipients (A-L)" http://www.history.army.mil/html/moh/civwaral.html.
13. Ibid.
14. "38th United States Colored Troops."
15. Ibid.
16. Ibid; Ralston.
17. Todd; "38th United States Colored Troops;" "38th Regiment, United States Colored Infantry."

Chapter 4--- Powhatan Beaty
1. "Cincinnati Patriot or Black Union Hero." http://www.civilwarbummer.com/cincinnati-patriot-or-black-union-hero; "Powhatan Beaty, born October 8, 1837." http://civilwaref/blogspot.com/2013/10/powhatan-beaty-born-october-8-1837.html; Daut, Marlene. L. "Beaty, Powhatan." http://www.academia.edu/12864035/_Powhatan_Beaty_from_African_American_National_Biography; "A Colored Author and Actor." *The Indianapolis Leader*. Indianapolis, IN. January 15, 1881.
2. "Powhatan Beaty...1837."
3. Ibid.
4. Ibid; "Cincinnati...Hero."
5. Ibid.
6. "Powhatan Beaty...1837."
7. Talbot, Tim. "Fort Wright: The Black Brigade." http://explorekyhistory.ky.gov /items/ show/96?tour=9&index=21.
8. "Cincinnati...Hero;" "Powhatan Beaty...1837."
9. "Cincinnati...Hero;" Gorman, Ron. "The Battle of New Market Heights: the 5th USCT's 'Glory.' http://www.Oberlinheritagecenter.org/blog/2014/09/the-battle-of-new-market-heights-the-5th-uscts-glory/.
10. "Cincinnati...Hero;" "Powhatan Beaty...1837."
11. "Powhatan Beaty...1837."
12. Ibid; Schemmer, Clint. "Black soldiers 'silenced every cavil of the doubters.' http://www.Fredericksburg.com/features/black-soldiers-silenced-every-cavil-of-the-doubters/article_f31f9c29-3e16-59e3-ad39-e7e90af6f9b8.html.
13. "Powhatan Beaty...1837."
14. Ibid; Schemmer.
15. "Powhatan Beaty...1837."
16. Schemmer.
17. Ibid.
18. Ibid; Schemmer.
19. Schemmer.
20. Ibid.
21. "Powhatan Beaty...1837."
22. Ibid; "Cincinnati...Hero;" Marcois, Bart. "Powhatan Beaty: Hero, Engineer, Actor, Playwright, Father." https://www.Opslens.com/2018/02/02/powhatan-beaty-hero-black-history-month; "Abraham Lincoln." *The Cincinnati Daily Star*. Cincinnati, OH. February 13, 1878.
23. "Cincinnati...Hero;" "Powhatan Beaty...1837;" Jones, Jae. "Powhatan Beaty: Actor & Soldier Decorated with United States Medal of Honor." n.d.; "Delmar, or Scenes in Southland." *The Weekly*

Louisianan. New Orleans. March 27, 1880; "Ford's Opera House." *The Bee.* Washington, D. C. May 3, 1884.
24. "Powhatan Beaty...1837;" "Cincinnati...Hero."
25. Ibid.
26. "Powhatan Beaty...1837."
27. "Cincinnati...Hero;" Today in Black History 12/6/2011.http://thewright.org/explore/ exhibitions/581 -witness-the-art-of-jerry-pinkney; "Powhatan Beaty is Dead." *The Labor Advocate.* Cincinnati, Ohio. December 6, 1916.
28. "Powhatan Beaty...1837."

Chapter 5---Robert Blake
1. Jones, Jae. "Robert Blake: Union Navy Sailor During the American Civil War." January 23, 2018. https://blackthen.com/robert-blake-union-navy-sailor-american-civil-war. Accessed March 21, 2018; "Robert Blake: Slave, Contraband, Sailor, and Hero." https://markerhunter.wordpress.com/2013/12/26/robert-blake. Accessed March 21, 2013.
2. "Robert Blake...Hero."
3. "Blake's County." https://south-carolina-plantations-com/charleston/blakes.html. Accessed April 3, 2018.
4. Jones, Jae. "Robert...Civil War;" "Robert Blake...Hero."
5. "USS Marblehead." http://www.navsource.org/archives/09/86/86330.htm. Accessed April 2, 2018; Walker, Richard. "Ex-slave, Medal of Honor recipient, remembered with naming of DMV." http://thetandd.com/news/local/ex-slave-medal-of-honor-recipient-remembered-with-naming-of/article_cc2bea50-519b-11e3-a886-001a4bcf887a.html. Accessed April 2, 2018.
6. Walker, Richard. "Ex-slave...DMV:" "USS Marblehead;" Jones. Jae. "Robert Blake...Hero."
7. Ibid.
8. Walker, Richard. "Ex-slave...DMV:" "USS Marblehead:" "Meade to Dahlgren, *ORN,* 15:190-191.
9. "Meade to Dahlgren;" Miles, Suzannah Smith. "Legareville once a happy, summer village." https://www.moultrienews.com/archives/legareville-once-a-happy-summer-village/article_be3a11d6-655a-5cb7-acd7-507702e8402f.html. Accessed April 2, 2018; "Blake, Robert." themedalofhonor.com. Accessed November 24, 2018.
10. "Blake, Robert." themedalofhonor.com.
11. Jones, Jae. "Robert Blake...Hero;" "Who was the first black person to win the congressional Medal of Honor?" https://socratic.org/questions/who-was-the-first-black-person-to-win-the-congressional-medal-of-honor. Accessed April 3, 2018.

12. Walker, Richard. "Ex-slave...DMV;" Jones, Jae. "Robert Blake...Hero."
13. Walker, Richard. "Ex-slave...DMV."
14. Miles, Suzannah Smith. "Legareville...village."

Chapter 6---James Bronson
1. Nichols, Ben. "James H. Bronson." http://ranger95.com/civil_war_us/us_color_troops/infantry/5usct/james_h_bronson_d_5usct.htm. Accessed April 4, 2018; Sagely, Pamela. "Two Indiana County veterans to be inducted into Hall of Valor." http://triblive.com/news/Indiana/5747360-74/prola-valor-hall. Accessed April 4, 2018; "Bronson, James H." https://www.nps.gov/rich/learn/historyculture/bronson.htm. Accessed April 3, 2018. Bearss, Edwin C. "Black Medals of Honor Received at New Market Heights, 29 September 1864." National Park Service memo in Richmond NBP files. 2 April 1979; Fijalkovich, Jessica. "James H. Bronson." https://sites.google.com/a/kent.edu/genealogy-local-history-2015/Jessica-fij/james-h-bronson. Accessed April 4, 2018.
2. Ibid.
3. Nichols. "James H. Bronson;" Virginia Foundation for the Humanities. "Richmond National Battlefield Park and Medal of Honor Monument." http://www.aahistoricsitesva.org/items/show/360?tour=3&index=6. Accessed April 3, 2016.
4. Virginia Foundation...Humanities; "On the Battlefield." https://www.nps.gov/park history/online_books/civil_war_series/2/sec18.htm. Accessed April 4, 2018; Mangus, Mike. "5th Regiment United States Colored Troops (1861-1865.) http://www.ohiocivilwar central.com/entry.php?rec=749. Accessed April 4, 2018.
5. Nichols. "James H. Bronson."
6. Ibid.
7. Ibid; "Bronson, James H."
8. Nichols. "James H. Bronson."
9. "James H. Bronson." https://valormilitarytimes.com. Accessed April 3, 2018.
10. Ibid; Sagely.
11. Ibid.
12. Nichols. "James H. Bronson."
13. Ibid; Fijalkovich.
14. Nichols. "James H. Bronson."
15. Sagely.
16. Nichols. "James H. Bronson;" "1SGT James H. Bronson." https://www.findagrave.com/ memorial/7218078/james-h.-bronson. Accessed April 3, 2018.

17. Sagely.

Chapter 7—William Brown
1. The Greater Atlanta Buffalo Soldiers. "William H. Brown-Medal of Honor." https://www.facebook.com/permalink.php?id=1533332710226719&story_fbid=1692271397666182. Accessed April 5, 2018.
2. Silverstone, Paul H. *Warships of the Civil War Navies*. Naval Institute Press. Annapolis, MD. 1989; *The New York Times*. January 15, 1858.
3. The Greater Atlanta Buffalo Soldiers.
4. Ibid; "CSS Tennessee." https://americancivilwar.com/tcwn/civil_war/Navy_Ships/CSS_Tennessee.html. Accessed April 5, 2018.
5. The Greater Atlanta; Medal of Honor Recipients—Civil War (A-L). http://www.history.army.mil/moh/civwaral.html. Accessed April 5, 2018; Medal of Honor Recipients—Civil War (M-Z). http://www.history.army.mil/moh/civwarmz.html. Accessed April 5, 2018.
6. The Greater Atlanta; Patterson, Michael Robert. "William H. Brown." http://www.Arlingtoncemetery.nat/whbrown.htm. Accessed April 5, 2018; "William H. Brown." https:www/findagrave.com/memorial/18821/william-h.-brown. Accessed April 5, 2018.
7. Ibid.

Chapter 8—Wilson Brown
1. The Wright Blogger. "Today in Black History: 1/24/2014." https://thewright.org/ index.php/explore/educational-resources/2013-11-27-37/today-in-black-history-1242014; Daut, Marlene. "Brown, Wilson." http://www.academia.edu/12864121/_Wilson_Brown_from_African_American_National_Biography; McRae, Bennie. "Resting Place of Landsman Wilson Brown and hundreds Union Army/Navy Civil War soldiers and sailors." lestweforget.hamptonu.edu/page.cfm?uuid=9FEC3293-E6EC-61F1-958D30F235422C4F; McRae, Bennie, "Union Navy: Wilson Brown and Tom Gates." www.afrigeneas.com/forum-militaryarchive/archive/index.cgi/md/read/id/720 /sbj/union-navy-wilson-brown-and-tom-gates.
2. Demby; McRae, Union Navy.
3. Daut, "Brown, Wilson;" Katz, William Loren. "Six New Medal of Honor Men: William H. Brown, Wilson Brown, William Loren Katz, Adam Paine." *Journal of Negro History*. January 1968. 77.

4. The Wright Blogger. "Today in Black History;" Hanna, Charles W. *African American recipients of the Medal of Honor: a biographical dictionary, Civil War through Vietnam War.* McFarland and Company, Inc., 2010, 21-22.
5. Burkett, Clark. "Brown awarded Medal of Honor nearly 100 years after Civil War." *Natchez Democrat.* February 11, 2009.
6. Ibid; The Wright Blogger. "Today in Black History;" "West Gulf Blockading Squadron." https://www.nps.gov/wicr/learn/historyculture/brown-navy.htm.
7. Daut, "Brown, Wilson;" "Wilson Brown: Medal of Honor recipient."http://enacademic. com/dic.nsf/enwiki/4688343.
8. "Wilson Brown: Medal of Honor recipient."
9. Ibid.
10. Ibid; Wright Blogger. "Today in Black History."
11. Wright Blogger. "Today in Black History;" Burkett, Clark; "Wilson Brown." http://www.homeofheroes.com/gravesites/states/pages_af/brown_wilson_ms.html.
12. Burkett, Clark.
13. Ibid.
14. Wright Blogger; "Wilson Brown: Medal of Honor recipient;" Demby; McRae, "Resting Place;" McRae, "Union Navy."
15. Burkett.

Chapter 9—William Carney
1. Lange, Katie. "Meet Sgt. William Carney: The First African American Medal of Honor Recipient." DoD News, Defense Media Activity. n.p., n.d.; "Sgt. William Carney, Jr. (1840-1908) Medal of Honor Recipient." https://americacomesalive.com/2013/05/28/sgt-william-carney-jr-1840-1908-medal-of-honor-recipient; Helm, Matt. "Carney, William H." www.blackpast.org/aah/carney-william-h-1840-1908; Coddington, Ronald S. "The Old Flag Never Touched the Ground." *New York Times.* July 19, 2013. The Opinion Pages.
2. Opinde, Walter. "A Brave Black Man at the Warfront: Sergeant William Carney Harvey. [sic]" https: blackthen.com/brave-man-warfront-sergeant-william-carney-harvey.
3. Helm, "Carney…"
4. Hammond, Thomas M. "William H. Carney: 54th Massachusetts Soldier and First Black U. S. Medal of Honor Recipient." *America's Civil War.* January 29, 2007 n.p.
5. Helm, "Carney…;" Lange, "Meet Sgt. William Carney…"
6. Helm, "Carney…;" Opinde, "A Brave Black Man…"
7. Helm, "Carney…;" Coddington, "The Old Flag…"

8. Pohanka, Brian C. "Fort Wagner and the 54th Massachusetts Volunteer Infantry." https://www.civilwar.org/learn/articles/fort-wagner-and-54th-massachusetts-volunteer-infantry.
9. Hammond, "William H. Carney…"
10. Coddington, "The Old Flag…"
11. Ibid; Helm, "Carney…"
12. Ibid.
13. Coddington, "The Old Flag…"
14. Ibid
15. Ibid.
16. Ibid.
17. Ibid.
18. Ibid; Helm, "Carney…"
19. Coddington, "The Old Flag…"
20. Hammond, "William H. Carney…"
21. Ibid; Helm, "Carney…;" Coddington, "The Old Flag…"
22. Ibid.
23. Opinde, "A Brave Black Man…;" "William H. Carney at Fort Wagner."Housedivided.dickinson.edu/grandreview/2010/06/04/william-h-carney-at-fort-wagner; "William H. Carney: First Black American to merit the Medal of Honor." Kentakepage.com/william-h-carney-first-black-american-to-merit-the-medal-of-honor.
24. "Sgt. William Carney, Jr. (1840-1908) Medal of Honor Recipient." https://americacomesalive. com/2013/05/28/sgt-william-carney-jr-1840-1908-medal-of-honor-recipient.
25. Coddington, "The Old Flag…;" Helm, "Carney…;" Hammond, "William H. Carney…;" Patrick, Bethanne Kelly. "Sgt. William H. Carney."https://www.military.com/history/sgt-william-h-carney.html; "Sgt. William Carney, Jr. (1840-1908) Medal of Honor Recipient." https://americacomesalive.com.
26. "Sgt. William Carney…Recipient;" "SGT William Harvey Carney." https://findagrave. com/memorial/6826582/william-harvey-carney; Helm, "Carney…;" Patrick, "Sgt. William H. Carney."

Chapter 10---Clement Dees
1. www.peachamhistorical.org/wpcontent/uploads/2016/06/PHA_Patriot_Summer_2011.pdf; www.racetimeplace.com/medalofhonor.htm.
2. Ibid.
3. "African American Recipients of the Medal of Honor: A Biographical Dictionary, Civil War through Vietnam War." https://eakumentasi.firebaseapp.com/african-american-recipients-of-the-medal-of-honor-a-biographical-dictionary-civil-war-through-vietnam-

war-jxjlkbej.html; "City Council Minutes 05/12/03."
http://www/eastport-me.gov/Public_Documents/EastportME_CouncilMin/2003/S001D13EE; "Navy Medals Rescinded."
http://www.homeofheroes.com/moh/corrections/purge_navy.html.

Chapter 11---Decatur Dorsey
1. Stern, Nicholas C. "Local family commemorates Civil War hero." *Frederick News-Post*.
2. Frederick, Maryland. August 17, 2008; "Decatur Dorsey." https://www.nps.gov/
3. learn/historyculture/decatur-dorsey.htm; Dorsey, Maurice H. "Hometown of Decatur Dorsey." https://www.hmdb.org/marker.asp?marker=5756; Sandoval, Timothy. "Church holds presentation on African-American contributions to the Civil War." *Carroll County Times*. Westminster, Maryland. February 24, 2014; Wordbone. "Tales of Two Cities." http://writing-the-wrongs.blogspot.com/2011/05/decatur-dorsey.html.
4. "Decatur Dorsey." https.www.nps.gov; "Decatur Dorsey, biography." http://www.fampeople.com/cat-decatur-dorsey; "Enlistment bounty paid to Edward Rider, Jr. for his slave Decatur Dorsey, October 26, 1864-January 13, 1866." https:// digital.lib.umd.edu/image?pid=umd:71368.
5. "United States Colored Troops: 39th Regiment, United States Colored Infantry." https://www.nps.gov/civilwar/search-battle-units-detail.htm?battleUnitCode =UUS0039RI00C.
6. https://www.nps.gov/pete/learn/historyculture/the-crater.htm; Acocella, Nicholas. "Famous Hobokenites: Decatur Dorsey Civil War sergeant from Hoboken won Medal of Honor. *Hudson Reporter*. September 13, 2005.
7. https://www.nps.gov/pete; Chandler, D. L. "Former Slave, Medal of Honor Recipient Rallied Colored Soldiers 148 Years Ago Today." https://newsone.com/2027758/decatur-dorsey-medal-of-honor.
8. Acocella; "Decatur Dorsey, biography." http://www.fampeople.com; Sandoval; Wordbones; "Decatur Dorsey." https://www.historicalmarkerproject.com/ markers/view.php?marker_id=HM3BP.
9. Wordbones.
10. Sandoval.
11. Wordbones.
12. "Decatur Dorsey." https://valor.militarytimes.com/hero/635.
13. United States Colored Troops: 39th Regiment, United States Colored Infantry." https://www.nps.gov.
14. "Decatur Dorsey." https://www.nps.gov; "Decatur Dorsey, biography." http://www.fampeople.com; Murray, Shannon D. "Civil

War novelist conveys 'real story' of black soldiers through life of local hero." *Baltimore Sun.* July 17, 1994.
15. Ibid; Acocella; "National Guard Militia Museum of New Jersey." https://www.facebook.com/127004387321616/photos/pb.127004387321616.-2207520000. 1469301694./1131412973547414/?type=3.
16. Murray, "Civil War novelist;" Stern, Nicholas C. "Local family commemorates Civil War hero." *Frederick News-Post.* Frederick, Maryland. August 17, 2008; "Today in Black History, 7/11/2012." https://www.thewright.org/index.php/explore/educational-
17. resources/2013-11-28-11-27-37/today-in-black-history-7112012.

Chapter 12—Christian Fleetwood
1. "Christian Fleetwood." https://www.civilwar.org/learn/biographies/christian-fleetwood; Clifford, James H. "Sergeant Major Christian Fleetwood." https://armyhistory.org/sergeant-major-christian-fleetwood.
2. Ibid; Lewis, David. "Fleetwood, Christian Abraham." http://www.blackpast.org/aah /fleetwood-christian-abraham-1840-1914; "Christian Fleetwood: And Now.....For the Rest of the Story." http://www.stevenson.edu/academics/undergraduate- programs/public-history/blog-news-events/Christian-fleetwood-and-now-for-the-rest-of-the-story.
3. "Christian Fleetwood." www.civilwar.org; Lewis, "Fleetwood...;" Clifford, "Sergeant...Fleetwood;" Bock, James. "Witnessing history, Read on: Students are immersed in the Civil War heroics and struggles of a black soldier from Baltimore; an attempt to whet their appetite for books." *Baltimore Sun.* March 4, 1996. n.p.
4. Talbot, Tim. "Personality Spotlight: Christian Fleetwood." http://randomthoughtsonhistory.blogspot.com/2017/11/personality-spotlight-christian.html.
5. "Christian Fleetwood." www.civilwar.org; Lewis, "Fleetwood...;" Bock, "Witnessing history...;" Clifford, "Sergeant...Fleetwood."
6. "Christian Fleetwood," www.civilwar.org; "Fleetwood, Christian A." https://www.nps.gov/rich/learn/historyculture/fleetwood.htm.
7. Clifford, "Sergeant...Fleetwood."
8. Carey, John E. "Christian Fleetwood: Medal of Honor." https://civilwarstoriesofinspiration.wordpress.com/2008/09/20/Christian-fleetwood-medal-of-honor.
9. Ibid.
10. Clifford, "Sergeant...Fleetwood."
11. Whitacre, Paula Tarnapol. "Sgt. Major Christian Fleetwood: USCT Member, Medal of Honor Recipient, Diary Keeper. http://www.paulawhitacre.com/blog/ 2017/9/13/christian.fleetwood.

12. Lewis, "Fleetwood…"
13. Ibid; Bock, "Witnessing history…;" Talbot, Tim. "Personality Spotlight…;" "4th U. S. C. T. National Flag made by the 'Colored Ladies of Baltimore' Carried In The Battle Of New Market Heights in 1864." n.d.
14. Carey, "Christian Fleetwood…"
15. "Christian Fleetwood's Medal of Honor." https://www.civilwar.org/learn/primary-sources/christian-fleetwoods-medal-honor; Sicher, Peter A. "The African American Heroes of New Market Heights." https://www.civilwar.org/learn/articles/ covered-glory.
16. "Christian…Medal of Honor," civilwar.org.
17. Ibid.
18. Ibid.
19. Ibid.
20. Clifford, "Sergeant…Fleetwood."
21. "Christian Fleetwood," civilwar.org; "Christian…Medal of Honor," civilwar.org; Sicher, "The African American…Heights."
22. "Christian Fleetwood," civilwar.org.
23. "Christian A. Fleetwood. Letter of June 8, 1865."
24. Talbot, "Personality Spotlight…"
25. Ibid; "Christian Fleetwood," civilwar.org; "Christian Fleetwood, Officer and promoter of Black military groups." https://aaregistry.org/story/ Christian-fleetwood-officer-and-promoter-of-black-miliatry-groups; Clifford, "Sergeant…Fleetwood."
26. Clifford, "Sergeant…Fleetwood."
27. "Christian Fleetwood," civilwar.org; "Christian Fleetwood…military groups," aaregistry.org.
28. "Christian Fleetwood's Medal of Honor."https://amhistory.si.edu/military/ collection/object.asp?ID=417; Whitacre, "Sgt. Major Christian Fleetwood…"
29. "Christian Fleetwood…military groups," aaregistry.org.
30. Ibid; "Christian Fleetwood…Story," Talbot, "Personality Spotlight..;" "Christian Fleetwood," civilwar.org.
31. "Fleetwood's Testimonial." *The Washington Bee*. Washington, D. C. February 2, 1889.
32. Ibid.
33. Ibid.
34. Ibid.
35. Ibid.
36. "Christian Fleetwood…military groups," "Christian Fleetwood…Story," Talbot, "Personality Spotlight..;" "Christian Fleetwood," civilwar.org.
37. Ibid; "Christian Fleetwood and Sara Fleetwood Residence Site." https:/ /www. hmdb.org/marker.asp?marker=77543.

38. "Christian Fleetwood...Site," www.hmdb.org; "Death Record. Fleetwood, Christian A." Evening Star. Washington, D. C. September 30, 1914.
39. "Christian Fleetwood...military groups," aaregistry.org; Ibid.
40. Ibid; "Fleetwood, Christian A." https://www.nps.gov/rich/learn/historyculture/ fleetwood.htm; "Christian Fleetwood," civilwar.org; Talbot, "Personality Spotlight..." "Medal of Honor: Christian A. Fleetwood." http://www.civilwar.si.edu/soldiering_medal_of_honor.html.

Chapter 13---James Gardiner
1. Price, Jimmy. "Profile in Courage: Sgt. James Gardner, Co. I 36th USCT." http://sablearm.blogspot.com/2010/08/profile-in-courage-sgt-james-gardner-co.html; "James Daniel Gardner." https://www.findagrave.com/memorial/7661519/james-daniel-gardner.
2. Price, "Profile...;" "Gardiner, James."https://www.nps.gov/rich/learn/historyculture/ gardiner.htm.
3. "36th U.S. Colored Infantry Medal of Honor Winners." http://www.ncgenweb.us/ncusct/ medals.htm; "United States Colored Troops: 36th Regiment Infantry." https://www.nps.gov/rich/learn/historyculture/36thusct.htm.
4. Price, "Profile..."
5. Ibid
6. Ibid.
7. *OR*, Ser. 1, v. XLII, pt. 1, 819.
8. Ibid.
9. Price, "Profile...;" "36th U.S. Colored Infantry Medal of Honor Winners." http://www.ncgenweb.us.
10. "36th U.S. Colored Infantry Medal of Honor Winners." http://www.ncgenweb.us.
11. Ibid.
12. "Gardiner, James." http://www.homeofheroes.com/moh/citations_1862_cwa/gardiner_ james.html; *OR*, Ser. 1, v. XLII, pt. 1, 168.
13. Price, "Profile..."
14. Ibid; "United States Colored Troops: 36th Regiment Infantry."
15. "United States Colored Troops: 36th Regiment Infantry;" "Iowa Civil War Monuments." http://www.iowacivilwarmonuments.com/cgi-bin/gaard-details.pl?1227230506-2.
16. Stewart, Selma. "USCT James Daniel Gardner Honored." *Daily Press*, Newport News, VA. May 25, 2006.

Chapter 14: James Harris

1. "James H. Harris." http://www.arlingtoncemetery.net/jhharris.htm; "United States Colored Troops (USCT) Civil War Memorial Monument." https://www.
2. ucaconline.org/historic-monuments-and-statues.html; "Harris, James H." https://www.nps.gov/rich/learn/historyculture/harris.htm.
3. Hanna. 35-36.
4. "Richmond National Battlefield Park and Medal of Honor Monument." http://www.aahistoricsitesva.org/items/show/360?tour=3&index=6.
5. Ibid.
6. "James H. Harris." http://www.arlingtoncemeterynet; "SGT James H. Harris." https://www.findagrave.com/memorial/18822/james-h.-harris.
7. "Harris, James H. https://www.nps.gov.
8. Ibid.
9. "James H. Harris." http://www.arlingtoncemetery.net; "United States Colored Troops... Monument;" "Harris, James H." www.nps.gov; "SGT James H. Harris;" www.findagrave.com; Mumper, Wes. "Col. David L. Stricker Camp #64 SUVCW Delaware." https://www.facebook.com/stricker-suvcw/posts/726225370778418; "Ground Breaking for U.S. Colored Troop Memorial Monument, March 4, 2012, in Lexington
10. Park, Maryland." https://jubiloemancipationcentry.wordpress.com/tag/sgt-james-h-harris.

Chapter 15: Thomas Hawkins
1. "Sgt Maj Thomas R. Hawkins."https://www.findagrave.com/memorial/7101904/_thomas-r.-hawkins.
2. "Thomas R. Hawkins." http://philadelphiaencyclopedia.org/3c18559r-2; Price, Jimmy. "Profile in Courage: Sergeant-Major Thomas R. Hawkins, 6th USCT." http://
3. sablearm.blogspot.com/2010/06/profile-in-courage-sergeant-major.html; "Thomas R. Hawkins." https://www.hmdb.org/marker.asp?marker=74789.
4. Price, "Profile...Hawkins, 6th USCT."
5. Ibid.
6. Colimore, Edward. "New painting honors key Civil War moment for African Americans." http://bobandrewsgroup.com/new-painting-honors-key-civil-war-moment-for-african-americans.
7. Price, "Profile...Hawkins, 6th USCT."
8. "Three Medals of Honor—by Don Troiani." http://www.framingfox.com/ tmeofhobycoh.html.
9. Price, "Profile...Hawkins, 6th USCT."
10. Ibid.

11. Ibid.
12. Ibid; "Sgt Maj Thomas R. Hawkins." findagrave.com.
13. Ibid; "Died." *The Evening Star*. Washington, D. C. March 1, 1870. p. 3.
14. Price, "Profile...Hawkins, 6th USCT."
15. Ibid; "Died;" "Sgt Maj Thomas R. Hawkins." findagrave.com; Harris, Hamil R., Smith, Leef. "On Memorial Day, Soldiers and Citizens Honor Sacrifices of
16. Those Who Fought for Freedom." *The Washington Post*. May 27, 1997. p. B12.
17. "Three Medals of Honor;" Colimore, "New painting...;" "Thomas R. Hawkins," philadelphiaencyclopedia.com.

Chapter 16:   Alfred Hilton
1. "Alfred B. Hilton: Medal of Honor Recipient." https://www.mhdb.org/market.asp? marker=92020; "Hilton, Alfred B." https://www.nps.gov/rich/learn/historyculture /hilton.htm; Vought, Allan. "Alfred Hilton, Harford's only Medal of Honor recipient." http://www.baltimoresun.com.news/maryland/harford/aegis/retro-alfred-hilton- 20161104-story.html.
2. Vought, Allan. "Alfred...;" "Alfred B. Hilton: Medal of Honor Recipient."
3. Vought, Allan. "Alfred...:"
4. Ibid.
5. "Alfred B. Hilton: Medal of Honor Recipient."
6. Ibid; "Hilton, Alfred B.;" Vought, Allan. "Alfred..."
7. "Alfred B. Hilton: Medal of Honor Recipient."
8. Ibid.
9. Sturgill, Erika Quesenbery. "Alfred Hilton: Harford's Medal of Honor recipient." http://www.cecildaily.com/barganeer/alfred-hilton-harford-s-medal-of-honor-recipient/article_ c46d73b8-b469-5d7d-8b4e-6b03e16c7acc.html.
10. Ibid; Mainstd. "Unsung authors at the Historical Society of Harford County." http://www.belairartsandentertainment.org/2014/01/14/2545.
11. O.R., Ser. I, v. 89, p. 169.
12. "Hilton, Alfred B.;" Mainstd; "SGT Alfred B. Hilton;" https://www.findagrave.com/ memorial/7895145/alfred.b.hilton.
13. "Hilton, Alfred B.;" Sturgill, Erika Quesenberry. "Alfred..."
14. Vought, Allan. "Alfred..."
15. Ibid; Sturgill, Erika Quesenberry. "Alfred...;" "Alfred B. Hilton Park." http://www.harfordcountymd.gov/Facilities/Facility/Details/Alfred-B-Hilton-Park-4.

16. "Sgt. Alfred B. Hilton Bridge dedication set for Thursday, Nov. 9." http://www.baltimoresun.com/news/maryland/harford/aegis/ph-ag-hilton-bridge-dedication -preview-20171107-story.html.
17. Sparks, Cheryl M. "MDTA Dedicates MD 22 Bridge over 1-95 to Harford County Civil War Veteran." http://www.mdot.maryland.gov/News/Releases2017/2017_Nov_9_Bridge_Dedicated_to_Civil_War_Hero;" Johnson, Yvonne. "MD22 bridge memorializes Civil War Soldier, Harco Medal of Honor recipient." APG NEWS. November 16, 2017.
18. Vought, Allan. "Alfred…"

Chapter 17: Milton Holland
1. "Milton M. Holland." http://www.cemetery.state.tx.us/pub/user_form.asp?pers_id= 11147; Perdreau, Connie. "A Biographical Sketch of Master Sergeant Milton Holland." http: grosvenor-cwrt.org/our-moh-recipients/more-about-master-sergeant-milton-holland;
2. "Milton Holland, born August 1st, 1844." http://civilwaref.blogspot.com/2013/08/milton-holland-born-august-1st-1844.html.
3. Lucko, Paul M. "Holland, Milton M." https://tshonline.org/handbook/online/articles. fhobt; Cutrer, Thomas W. "Holland, Bird." https://tshaonline.org/handbook/online/ articles/fho22; Ratcliffe, Robert. "The Sons of Bird Holland." http://ratcliffe.com/Sonsof BirdHolland/category/bird-holland.
4. Lucko, Paul M. "Holland..;" Cutrer, Thomas W. "Holland..;" Perdreau, Connie. "A Biographical…"
5. Lucko, Paul M. "Holland..;" Cutrer, Thomas W. "Holland..;" "Milton M. Holland." http://www.cemetery.state.tx.us.
6. Perdreau, Connie. "A Biographical..;" "Milton M. Holland." http://www.cemetery. state.tx.us; *The Freeman*. Indianapolis, IN. December 7, 1889; McIlvain, Myra H. "Former Texas Slaves Serve in Civil War." https://myrahmcilvain.com/2013/
7. 12/20/former-texas-slaves-serve-in-civil-war.
8. Ibid.
9. Cutrer, Thomas W. "Holland..;" Ratcliff, Robert. "The Sons..;" "Milton Holland, born…"
10. "Milton M. Holland." http://www.cemetery.state.tx.us; McIlvain, Myra H. "Former…;" Perdreau, Connie. "A Biographical..;" Langston, John Mercer. *From the Virginia Plantation to the National Capitol.* Hartford, CT. 1894. pp. 213-214; "Milton M. Holland: Sergeant Major, United States Army." http://www.arlingtoncemetery.net/
11. mholland,htm.
12. "Milton M. Holland." http://www.cemetery.state.tx.us; "Milton M. Holland: Sergeant Major…"

13. Langston, John Mercer. *From the Virginia...* 214.
14. Perdreau. Connie. "A Biographical.;" "Milton M. Holland: Sergeant Major…"
15. *The Messenger*. Athens, Ohio. February 4, 1864.
16. "Milton M. Holland: Sergeant Major..;" "Milton Holland, born..;" "Black soldier was first native Texan to receive Medal of Honor." http://texasalmanac.com/topics/ history/black-soldier-was-first-native-texan-receive-medal-honor.
17. McIlvain, Myra H. "Former…"
18. Ibid; Perdreau, Connie. "A Biographical…"
19. O. R., # 89, p. 168.
20. "Milton Holland, born..;"
21. Ibid.
22. "Milton M. Holland: Sergeant Major...;" Lucko, Paul M. "Holland, Milton M.;" "Holland, Milton M." https://www.nps.gov/rich/learn/historyculture/holland.htm.
23. "Milton Holland, born.;"
24. "Holland Letter 1." http://www.nps.gov/rich/learn/historyculture.mhletter1.htm.
25. "Milton M. Holland: Sergeant Major…;" Lucko, Paul M. "Holland, Milton M.;" Perdreau, Connie. "A Biographical.;" "Black soldier was first native Texan…" McIlvain, Myra H. "Former…"
26. Ibid.
27. Ibid; "Milton Holland, born…;" *The Freeman*. Indianapolis, IN. December 7, 1889.
28. Hyman, Carolyn. "Holland, Spearman." *Handbook of Texas Online*. http:/www/tshonline.org/handbook/online/articles/fho28; "Milton M. Holland, a Civil War soldier, was the first Texan to be awarded the Medal of Honor." http: // hollandhistory.blogspot.com/2014/09/milton-m-holland-civil-war-soldier-was.html.
29. *The Freeman*. Indianapolis, IN. December 7, 1889.
30. Perdreau, Connie. "A Biographical…"
31. Ibid.
32. Ibid; "Milton M. Holland." http://www.cemetery.state.tx.us; Lucko, Paul M. "Holland.;" "Milton M. Holland: Sergeant Major."
33. "Historical Marker Honors Former Slave Who Raised Civil War Regiment." https://www.ohio-forum.com/2013/11/historical-marker-honors-former-slave-who -raised-civil-war-regiment.

Chapter 18: Miles James
1. "1SGT Miles James." https://www.findagrave.com/memorial/10212798/miles-james.
2. "Miles James enlisted." https://www.facebook.com/TheHstryMakers/posts/ 1326194834094895.

3. Talbot, Tim. "Corporal Miles James-A Superior Soldier." http://randomthoughtson history.blogspot.com/2017/10/corporal-miles-james-superior-soldier.html
4. Ibid.
5. "Miles James enlisted."
6. Talbot, Tim. "Corporal Miles…"
7. Ibid.
8. Ibid.
9. Ibid; OR, #89, 214.
10. OR, #89, 168.
11. "James, Miles." https://www.nps.gov/rich/learn/historyculture/james.htm.
12. "1SGT Miles James."
13. Talbot, Tim. "Corporal Miles…"
14. "1SGT Miles James;" "Miles James." https://billiongraves.com/grave/Miles-James/14524162.
15. Kimberlin, Joanne. "In Chesapeake, black soldiers' legacy not forgotten." https://pilotonline.com/news/article_cd4a231f-65f7-54db-b723- e101687d3597.html.

Chapter 19: Alexander Kelly

1. "1SGT Alexander Kelly." https://www.findagrave.com/memorial/7235834/alexander. kelly; Scott, Donald. "Alexander Kelly." http://pacivilwar150.com/ThroughPeople/ AfricanAmericans/AlexanderKelly.html; Jones, Jae. "Alexander Kelly: Awarded the Medal of Honor for Actions at the Battle of Chaffin's Farm in Virginia." https://blackthen.com/alexander-kelly-awarded-medal-honor-actions-battle-chaffins- farm-virginia; "Alexander Kelly." https://americancivilwar.com/colored/alexander_ kelly.html.
2. Jones, Jae. "Alexander Kelly;" Scott, Donald. "Alexander Kelly."
3. Ibid; "Alexander Kelly." https://americancivilwar.com.
4. Ibid.
5. Scott, Donald. "Alexander Kelly."
6. Ibid.
7. Ibid.
8. "1SGT Alexander Kelly;" Jones, Jae. "Alexander Kelly."
9. "6th Regiment U. S. Colored Troop, Company F." http://www.paroots.com/pacw/usct/6thusc/6thusctcof.html; Scott, Donald. "Alexander Kelly."
10. Jones, Jae. "Alexander Kelly;" Scott, Donald. "Alexander Kelly."
11. Scott, Donald. "Alexander Kelly."
12. Ibid; "6th Regiment U. S. Colored Troop, Company F."
13. Jones, Jae. "Alexander Kelly."

Chapter 20: John Lawson

1. "Heroes of Camden, New Jersey: Landsman John Lawson." http://www.dvrbs.com/ CW/CamdenCountyHeroes-JohnLawson.htm; "Lawnside Resident Pays Ultimate Respect to Hero." *Camden Courier Courier-Post*. February 22, 2004; "John Lawson: Sailor Aboard the U.S.S. Hartford." https://ncnwjax.wordpress.com/2015/02/03/
2. john-lawson-1837-1919-sailor-aboard-the-u-s-s-hartford; "John Henry Lawson." https://www.findagrave.com/memorial/7197017/john-henry-lawson.
3. "Heroes of Camden, New Jersey…"
4. "John Lawson: Sailor…Hartford;" Kienle, Polly. "Black Men in Navy Blue: John H. Lawson and William B. Gould." https://www.nps.gov/articles/lawson-and-gould.htm; "John Lawson." http://snowhillgenealogy.com/SecondSite/CWBLv8_1116113-o/p74.htm.
5. "John Lawson: Sailor…Hartford;" "Heroes of Camden, New Jersey…;" "History of Mr. Lawson." Program from April 24, 2004 ceremony for John H. Lawson at Mt. Peace Cemetery in Lawnside, NJ; Jenkins, Mark F. "MOH: Landsman John Lawson." https://civilwartalk.com/threads/moh-landsman-john-lawson.115657; "John H. Lawson, Medal of Honor Recipient." http://americanhistory.si.edu/collections/search/object/nmah_1438234; Vasquez, Ryan. "150th Anniversary of the Battle of Mobile Bay." n.d.
6. "Heroes of Camden, New Jersey…;" "History of Mr. Lawson;" "John Lawson: Sailor… Hartford;" "John H. Lawson, Medal of Honor…"
7. Vasquez, Ryan, "150th…;" "John Lawson: Sailor…Hartford."
8. Ibid; "Heroes of Camden, New…;" "John Lawson." http://snowhillgenealogy.com.
9. "Heroes of Camden, New…"
10. Ibid; Boyd, Herb. "Naval hero John Henry Lawson." New York Amsterdam News. February 5, 2016. n.p.
11. "John Lawson." http://snowhillgenealogy.com.
12. "Heroes of Camden, New…;" "Lawnside Resident…;" "John Henry Lawson." https:// www.findagrave.com.
13. "Medal of Honor Winners on the African American Civil War Memorial." http://www.
14. isisinform.com/medal-of-honor-winners-on-the-african-american-civil-war-memorial.
15. "*USS Hartford*: Civil War-Era Warship, Sinks at its Berth in Norfolk VA Navy Yard." http: www.burnpit.us/2014/11/uss-hartford-civil-war-era-warship-sinks-its-berth-norfolk-va-navy-yard.

Chapter 21: James Mifflin

1. "Engineer's Cook James Mifflin, USN." https://www.ibiblio.org/hyperwar/Online Library/photos/per-us/uspers-m/j-mifflin.htm; "James Mifflin." https://www.findagrave.com/memorial/11704845/james-mifflin.
2. "U.S.S. Brooklyn." http://www.navsourc.org/archives/09/86/86052.htm.
3. "Engineer's Cook James Mifflin, USN."
4. "James Mifflin." https://www.findagrave.com.
5. "Engineer's Cook James Mifflin, USN;" Curci, Jane. "African American Medal of Honor Winner James Mifflin." http://www.genealogy.com/forum/surnames/topics/mifflin/180.
6. "U.S.S. Brooklyn." http://www.navsour.org.
7. "James Mifflin." https://www.findagrave.com; "James Mifflin." https://www. peoplemaven.com/p/rG613w/james-mifflin; "USS Mifflin." https://www. navsource.org/archives/10/01/03207.htm.

Chapter 22: Joachim Pease

1. "Joachim Pease." https://www.findagrave.com/memorial/12791169/joachim-pease; Gilkes, Paul. "Joachim Pease Medal of Honor from Civil War on public display in Washington, D.C." https://www.coinworld.com/news/us-coins/2017/10/joachim-pease-congressional-medal-of-honor.all.htm.
2. Ibid; "Joachim Pease." https://howlingpixel.com/i-en/Joachim_Pease; Smith, Carletta. "June 19, 1864: The Battle of Cherbourg Occurs." https://blackthen.com/june-19, 1864-battle-cherbourg-occurs/; "Black Mariners: Historic and Contemporary." http://www.
3. blackmariners.com/civilwar.html.
4. "The Sloop of War, Kearsarge." http://www.warner.nh.us/ships.htm; Hirtle, John. "The Seacoast's Civil War Star." *Atlantic News Beach Guide, 2004.* Hampton, NH.
5. Gilkes, Paul. "Joachim…;" "Joachim Pease." https://howlingpixel.com; "Black Mariners:" Hirtle, John. "The Seacoast's…;" "The Battle of the *USS Kearsarge* and the *CSS Alabama*." Philadelphia Museum of Art.
6. "The Battle of the *USS Kearsarge*…;" Hirtle, John. "The Seacoast's…"
7. Gilkes, Paul. "Joachim…;" "Joachim Pease." https://howlingpixel.com; "Black Mariners."
8. Gilkes, Paul. "Joachim…;" "Joachim Pease." https://howlingpixel.com; Smith, Carletta. "June 19, 1864…"
9. "Joachim Pease." https://www.findagrave.com.
10. Gilkes, Paul. "Joachim…;" "Medal of Honor Winners on the American Civil War Memorial."
11. Gilkes, Paul. "Joachim…"

12. "Joachim Pease." https://www.findagrave.com.

Chapter 23: Robert Pinn
1. https://gozips.com/sports/2017/5/25/athletics-facilities-rifle.aspx; Margolis, Cyrene. "Robert A. Pinn: Distinguished service in war and peace." http://www.cantonrep.com/ article/20120430/News/304309861; "Pinn, Robert Alexander." http://www.blackpast. org/aah/pinn-robert-alexander-1843-1911.
2. Ibid.
3. "Pinn, Robert Alexander." http://www.blackpast.
4. https://gozips.com/sports; "Pinn, Robert." https://www.nps.gov/rich/learn/history culture/pinn.htm.
5. "Robert Pinn." https://www.hmdb.org/marker.asp?marker=61478.
6. "Pinn, Robert." https://www.nps.gov; "Pinn, Robert Alexander."
7. "127th Regiment Ohio Volunteer Infantry." https://ww.ohiocivilwarcentral.com/ entry.php?rec=790.
8. Ibid.
9. Ibid; "Pinn, Robert Alexander."
10. "Pinn's left hand." www.loc.gov/podcasts/african-american-passages/episode3.html; "Stark's Famous: Robert Pinn." http://www.indeonline.com/news/20161021/starks-famous-robert-pinn; "Robert Pinn." https://www.hmdb.org; "Pinn, Robert." https://www.
11. nps.gov.
12. OR, #89, 168.
13. Margolis, Cyrene. "Robert A. Pinn."
14. Ibid; "127th Regiment Ohio Volunteer Infantry;" "Pinn, Robert." https://www.nps.gov; "Pinn, Robert Alexander."
15. Ibid; "Pinn's left hand."
16. Margolis, Cyrene. "Robert A. Pinn;" Pinn, Robert Alexander;" "Stark's Famous...;" gozips.com.
17. "Stark's Famous...; gozips.com.
18. Margolis, Cyrene. "Robert A. Pinn;" "Pinn, Robert Alexander;" "Robert Pinn." https://www.hmdb.org; "1SGT Robert A. Pinn." https://www.findagrave.com/ memorial/7784503/robert-a.-pinn.
19. "Robert Pinn." https://www.hmdb.org,
20. "Ohio National Guard Photo Gallery." https://ong.ohio.gov/images/photo-galleries/2015-02.html.
21. gozips.com

Chapter 24: Edward Ratcliff
1. Heinatz, Stephanie. "Born a Slave, Bred a Soldier." http://www.dailypress.com/news/ black-history/dp-7654sy0jul26-story.html.
2. Ibid.
3. Ibid.

4. Ibid.
5. Ibid.
6. Ibid.
7. Ibid.
8. Heinatz, Stephanie. "Living With Ghosts." http://ww.dailypress.com/news/black-history/dp-medalj123jul23-story.html; Piggott, Mark O. "Civil War Hero Remembered at Yorktown Black History Month Celebration." *Navy News Service*. February 25, 2011.
9. Heinatz, Stephanie. "Living With Ghosts."
10. Heinatz, Stephanie. "With Great Gallantry." https://www.dailypress.com/news/black-history/dp-civilwar5jul26-story.html; "Ratcliff, Edward." https://www.nps.gov/rich/ learn/historyculture/ratcliff.htm.
11. Heinatz, Stephanie. "With Great Gallantry."
12. Ibid.
13. Ibid.
14. Ibid.
15. Ibid
16. Ibid.
17. OR, #89, 168.
18. "Ratcliff, Edward." https://www.nps.gov.
19. Ibid; Piggott, Mark O. "Civil War Hero…"
20. Ibid.
21. Piggott, Mark O. "Civil War Hero…;" Heinatz, Stephanie. "Changing Times and Failing Body." http://www.dailypress.com/news/black-history/dp-79099sy0jul29-story.html.
22. Heinatz, Stephanie. "Changing Times…"
23. Ibid.
24. Ibid.
25. Heinatz, Stephanie. "Living With Ghosts;" Heinatz, Stephanie. "Cheesecake Cemetery." http://www.dailypress.com/news/black-history/dp-71927sy0jul24-story.html; Heinatz, Stephanie. "Visiting Cheesecake Cemetery." https://www.dailypress.com/news/black-history/dp-77503sy0jul28-story.html.
26. Heinatz, Stephanie. "A Saga Set in Stone." http://www.dailypress.com/news/black-history/dp-77642sy0jul30-story.html; Heinatz, Stephanie. "A man's milestone." http://www.dailypress.com/news/black-history/dp-93354sy0aug06-story.html.

Chapter 25: Andrew Jackson Smith
1. Bowman, Andrew S. "Andrew Jackson Smith." http://lestweforget.hamptonu. edu/page.cfm?uuid=9FEC4F41-F9E6-0797-FFF8C82DB8BB2A09.; kentuckyguard. "Corporal Andrew Jackson Smith, Kentucky's only African-American Civil War Medal of Honor recipient.

http://kentuckyguard.dodlive.mil/2015/02/09/corporal-andrew-jackson-smith-kentuckys-only-african-american-civil-war-medal-of-honor-recipient
2. Ibid; Craig, Berry. "Old Time Kentucky: Andy Smith's long-delayed Medal of Honor was a wrong that was righted." http://www.kyforward.com/old-time-kentucky-andy-smiths-long-delayed-medal-of-honor-was-a-wrong-that-was-righted.
3. Ibid; "Andrew Jackson Smith: African-American Civil War Hero." http://kentakepage. com/andrew-jackson-smith.
4. Bowman.
5. kentuckyguard.
6. Ibid; Craig; "Andrew Jackson Smith, born September 3, 1843." http://civilwaref.blogspot
7. Bowman; Craig.
8. Ibid; "Andrew Jackson Smith…Hero."
9. Bowman.
10. Hamilton, Lowell D. "The Battle of Honey Hill, South Carolina." Nd.
11. kentuckyguard; "Andrew Jackson Smith…Hero:" "Smith, Andrew Jackson." http://www.cmohs.org/recipient-detail/1261/smith-andrew-jackson.php.; Wise, Stephen R. "Honey Hill, Battle of." http://www.scencyclopedia.org/sce/ entries/honey-hill-battle-of.
12. Hamilton, Lowell.
13. Ibid; Craig; Bowman.
14. Craig; Bowman; "Smith, Andrew Jackson." http://www.cmohs.org.
15. Hartwell, Alfred. "Personal Reminiscences of the Civil War. Paper Read Before Honolulu Social Club. 1903.
16. Wise; Hamilton.
17. Bowman; "Andrew Jackson Smith…Hero."
18. Bowman.
19. Craig; Andrew Jackson Smith…:" Rozen-Wheeler, Adam. "Smith, Andrew Jackson." http://www.blackpast.org/aah/smith-andrew-jackson-1843-1932.
20. "Andrew Jackson Smith…hero."
21. "SGT Andrew Jackson Smith." https: www.findagrave.com/memorial/8762808/andrew-jackson-smith.; kentuckyguard; Craig; Bowman; "Andrew Jackson Smith…Hero."
22. "Andrew Jackson Smith…1843."
23. Ibid; Bowman; Craig; kentuckyguard; Andrew Jackson Smith…hero."
24. Craig.
25. Ibid.
26. https://themedalofhonor.com/medal-of-honor-recipients/recipients/smith-andrew-civil-war; www.cmohs.org---smith, a j.

Chapter 26: Charles Veale
1. "PVT Charles Veale." https://www.findagrave.com/memorial/7895208/charles-veale.
2. Ibid; "Veal Charles." https://www.nps.gov/rich/learn/historyculture/veal.htm.
3. "Charles Veale, PVT." https://www.geni.com/people/Charles-Veale-PVT-USA/ 6000000012677094814; Regan, Christopher J. "The American flag, Medal of Honor and the President." http://www.montgomery-herald-com/opinion/the- american-flag-medal-of-honor-and-the-president/article_d74af260-a8bc-11e7-9701-93647d713c50html.
4. Ibid.
5. "PVT Charles Veale." https://www.findagrave.com; "Veal Charles." https://www.nps.
6. "Veal Charles" https://www.nps.; OR, #89, p. 169.
7. "During the day about thirty more men came along all." https://www.coursehero.com/ file/pv144v/During-the-day-about-thirty-more-men-came-along-all-that-was-left-I-have-never/; "Maryland Society to Display Rare USCT Flag." Baltimore Civil War Roundtable. Nd.
8. "PVT Charles Veale." https://www.findagrave.com; "Veal Charles" https://www.nps; "Today in Black History, 7/27/2014." https://thewright.org/index.php/explore/ educational-resources/2013-11-28-11-27-37/today-in-black-history-7272014

Bibliography

"Aaron Anderson." https://civilwarpvmhs.weebly.com/aaron-anderson.html Accessed May 10, 2018.

"Abraham Lincoln." *The Cincinnati Daily Star*. Cincinnati, OH. February 13, 1878.

Acocella, Nicholas. "Famous Hobokenites: Decatur Dorsey Civil War sergeant from Hoboken won Medal of Honor. *Hudson Reporter*. September 13, 2005.

"A Colored Author and Actor." *The Indianapolis Leader*. Indianapolis, IN. January 15, 1881.

"African-American private was a Civil War hero." http://www.wral.com/african-american-private-was-a-civil-war-hero/14368826/ Accessed March 20, 2018.

"African American Recipients of the Medal of Honor: A Biographical Dictionary, Civil War through Vietnam War." https://eakumentasi.firebaseapp.com/african-american-recipients-of-the-medal-of-honor-a-biographical-dictionary-civil-war-through-vietnam-war-jxjlkbej.html Accessed April 17, 2018.

"African Americans in the Armed Forces Timeline." https://www.civilwar.org/learn/articles/african-americans-armed-forces-timeline Accessed April 19, 2018.

"African-American Soldiers During the Civil War." http://www.loc.gov/teachers/classroom-Materials/presentationsandactivities/presentations/timeline/civilwar/aasoldrs/ Accessed March 20, 2018.

"Alexander Kelly." https://americancivilwar.com/colored/alexander_kelly.html Accessed April 10, 2018.

"Alfred B. Hilton: Medal of Honor Recipient." https://www.mhdb.org/market.asp?marker=92020 Accessed April 18, 2018.

"Alfred B. Hilton Park." http://www.harfordcountymd.gov/Facilities/Facility/Details/Alfred-B-Hilton-Park-4 Accessed April 18, 2018.

"Anderson, Aaron—Medal of Honor." http://historymugs.us/product/aaron-anderson-medal-of-honor/ Accessed March 20, 2018.

"Andrew Jackson Smith: African-American Civil War Hero." http://kentakepage.com/andrew-jackson-smith Accessed April 13, 2018.

"Andrew Jackson Smith, born September 3, 1843." http://civilwaref.blogspot Accessed April 13, 2018.

"Battle of Mattox Creek, Virginia." https://www.theclio.com/web/entry?id=47931 Accessed March 16, 2018.

"The Battle of the *USS Kearsarge* and the *CSS Alabama*." Philadelphia Museum of Art.

Bearss, Edwin C. "Black Medals of Honor Received at New Market Heights, 29 September 1864." National Park Service Memo in Richmond NBP files, 2 April 1979.

Berg, Gordon. "Battle of New Market Heights: USCT Soldiers Proved Their Heroism." *America's Civil War*. March 2006. Accessed March 16, 2018.

"Black History Month Highlight: Aaron Anderson." http://civilwarnavy150.blogspot.com/2011/02/black-history-month-highlight-aaron.html Accessed May 16, 2018.

"Black Mariners: Historic and Contemporary." http://www.blackmariners.com/civilwar.html Accessed April 19, 2018.

"Black soldier was first native Texan to receive Medal of Honor." http://texasalmanac.com/topics/history/black-soldier-was-first-native-texan-receive-medal-honor Accessed April 10, 2018.

"Black Troops in Union Blue." http://www.crf-usa.org/black-history-month/black-troops-in-blue Accessed March 20, 2018.

"Blake, Robert." themedalofhonor.com Accessed November 24, 2018.

"Blake's Plantation." https://south-carolina-plantations.com/charleston.blakes.html Accessed April 3, 2018.

Bock, James. "Witnessing history, Read on: Students are immersed in the Civil War heroics and struggles of a black soldier from Baltimore: an attempt to whet their appetite for books." *Baltimore Sun*. March 4, 1996. n.p.

Bowman, Andrew S. "Andrew Jackson Smith." http://lestweforget.hamptonu.edu/page.cfm?uuid=9FEC4F41-F9E6-0797-FFF8C82DB8BB2A09 Accessed April 13, 2018.

Boyd, Herb. "Naval hero John Henry Lawson." *New York Amsterdam News*. February 5, 2016.

n.p.

"Bronson, James H." https://www.nps.gov/rich/learn/historyculture/bronson.htm Accessed April 3, 2018.

"Bruce Anderson, War Hero." https://www.famousbirthdays.com/people/bruce-anderson.html Accessed March 20, 2018.

Burkett, Clark. "Brown awarded Medal of Honor nearly 100 years after Civil War." *Natchez Democrat*. February 11, 2009.

Cannon, Helen. "Medal of Honor for Fort Fisher Action." http://nccivilwarcenter.org/medal-honor-fort-fisher-action/ Accessed March 16, 2018.

Carey, John E. "Christian Fleetwood: Medal of Honor." https://civilwarstoriesofinspiration.wordpress.com/2008/09/20/Christian-fleetwood-medal-of-honor Accessed April 6, 2018.

Chaitin, Peter M., ed. *The Coastal War: Chesapeake to Rio Grande*. Alexandria, Va: Time-Life Books. 1984.

Chandler, D. L. "Former Slave, Medal of Honor Recipient Rallied Colored Soldiers 148 Years Ago Today." https://newsone.com/2027758/decatur-dorsey-medal-of-honor Accessed April 6, 2018.

"Charles Veale, PVT." https://www.geni.com/people/Charles-Veale-PVT-USA/6000000012677094814 Accessed April 16, 2018.

"Christian A. Fleetwood." https://valor.militarytimes.com/hero/49 Accessed April 6, 2018.

"Christian A. Fleetwood. Letter of June 8, 1865."

"Christian Fleetwood." https://www.civilwar.org/learn/biographies/christian-fleetwood Accessed April 6, 2018.

"Christian Fleetwood: And Now.....For the Rest of the Story." http://www.stevenson.edu/academics/undergraduate-programs/public-history/blog-news-events/Christian-fleetwood-and-now-for-the-rest-of-the-story Accessed April 17, 2018.

"Christian Fleetwood and Sara Fleetwood Residence Site." https://www.hmdb.org/marker.asp?marker=77543 Accessed April 6, 2018.

"Christian Fleetwood, Officer and promoter of Black military groups." https://aaregistry.org/story/Christian-fleetwood-officer-and-promoter-of-black-miliatry-groups Accessed April 6, 2018.

"Christian Fleetwood's Medal of Honor." https://amhistory.si.edu/military/collection/object.asp?ID=417 Accessed April 6, 2018.

"Christian Fleetwood's Medal of Honor." https://www.civilwar.org/learn/primary-sources/christian-fleetwoods-medal-honor Accessed April 6, 2018.

"Cincinnati Patriot or Black Union Hero." http://www.civilwarbummer.com/cincinnati-patriot-or-black-union-hero Accessed March 21, 2018.

"City Council Minutes 05/12/03." http://www/eastport-me.gov/Public_Documents/EastportME_CouncilMin/2003/S001D13EE. Accessed April 117, 2018.

"Civil War Medal of Honor recipients (A-L)" http://www.history.army.mil/html/moh/civwaral.html Accessed March 16, 2018.

Civil War Soldiers and Sailors System. National Park Service. Archived from the original http://www.itd.nps.gov/cwss/regiments.cfm Accessed March 16, 2018.

Clifford, James H. "Sergeant Major Christian Fleetwood." https://armyhistory.org/sergeant-major-christian-fleetwood Accessed April 6, 2018.

Coddington, Ronald S. "The Old Flag Never Touched the Ground." *New York Times*. July 19, 2013. The Opinion Pages.

Colimore, Edward. "New painting honors key Civil War moment for African Americans." http://bobandrewsgroup.com/new-painting-honors-key-civil-war-moment-for-african-americans. Accessed April 16, 2018.

"Colored Troops in the American Civil War." https://americancivilwar.com/colored/colored_troops.html. Accessed April 19, 2018.

Craig, Berry. "Old Time Kentucky: Andy Smith's long-delayed Medal of Honor was a wrong that was righted." http://www.kyforward.com/old-time-kentucky-andy-smiths-long-delayed-medal-of-honor-was-a-wrong-that-was-righted Accessed April 13, 2018.

"*CSS Tennessee.*" https://americancivil-war.com/tcwn/civil_war/Navy_Ships/CSS_Tennessee.html Accessed April 5, 2018.

Cudmore, Bob. "Storming Fort Fisher during the Civil War." https://dailyga-zette.com/article/2014/09/13/storming-fort-fisher-during-civil-war Accessed March 16, 2018.

Curci, Jane. "African American Medal of Honor Winner James Mifflin." http://www.genealogy.com/forum/surnames/topics/mifflin/180 Accessed April 12, 2018.

Cutrer, Thomas W. "Holland, Bird." https://tshaonline.org/hand-book/online/articles/fho22 Accessed April 10, 2018.

Daut, Marlene. L. "Beaty, Powhatan." http://www.aca-demia.edu/12864035/_Powhatan_Beaty_from_African_American_National_Biography Accessed March 21, 2018.

----. "Brown, Wilson." http://www.academia.edu/12864121/_Wilson_Brown_from_African_American_National_Biography Accessed April 5, 2018.

"Death Record. Fleetwood, Christian A." *Evening Star*. Washington, D. C. September 30, 1914.

"Decatur Dorsey." https://www.historicalmarkerproject.com/mark-ers/view.php?marker_id=HM3BP Accessed April 6, 2018.

"Decatur Dorsey." https://www.nps.gov/pete/learn/historyculture/decatur-dorsey.htm Accessed April 6, 2018.

"Decatur Dorsey." https://valor.militarytimes.com/hero/635 Accessed April 6, 2018.

"Decatur Dorsey, biography." http://www.fampeople.com/cat-decatur-dorsey Accessed January 2, 2019.

"Delmar, or Scenes in Southland." *The Weekly Louisianan*. New Orleans. March 27, 1880.

Demby, Devonte. "Natchez man, Medal of Honor recipient having story told in project." *Natchez Democrat*. December 21, 2014.

"Died." *The Evening Star*. Washington, D. C. March 1, 1870. p. 3.

Dorsey, Maurice H. "Hometown of Decatur Dorsey." https://www.hmdb.org/marker.asp?marker=5756 Accessed April 6, 2018.

"During the day about thirty more men came along all." https://www.course-hero.com/file/pv144v/During-the-day-about-thirty-more-men-came-along-all-that-was-left-I-have-never/ Accessed April 16, 2018.

"Engineer's Cook James Mifflin, USN." https://www.ibiblio.org/hyper-war/OnlineLibrary/photos/per-us/uspers-m/j-mifflin.htm Accessed April 12, 2018.

"Enlistment bounty paid to Edward Rider, Jr. for his slave Decatur Dorsey, October 26, 1864-January 13, 1866." https://digital.lib.umd.edu/im-age?pid=umd:71368 Accessed January 5, 2019.

Feber, Eric. "Medal of Honor winners to be recognized." *The Virginian-Pilot*. November 10, 2006. http://pilotonline.com/news/local/article_301af75e-d911-5d97-a92b-2e00602689-e8.html Accessed April 16, 2018.

Fijalkovich, Jessica. "James H. Bronson." https://sites.google.com/a/kent.edu/genealogy-local-history-2015/Jessica-fij/james-h-bronson Accessed April 4, 2018.

"1SGT Alexander Kelly." https://www.findagrave.com/memorial/7235834/alexander.kelly Accessed April 10, 2018.

"1SGT James H. Bronson." https://www.findagrave.com/memorial/7218078/james-h.-bronson Accessed April 3, 2018.

"1SGT Miles James." https://www.findagrave.com/memorial/10212798/miles-james Accessed April 10, 2018.

"1SGT Robert A. Pinn." https://www.findagrave.com/memorial/7784503/robert-a.-pinn Accessed April 13, 2018.

"Fleetwood, Christian A." https://www.nps.gov/rich/learn/historyculture/fleetwood.htm Accessed April 6, 2018.

"Fleetwood's Testimonial." *The Washington Bee*. Washington, D. C. February 2, 1889.

"Ford's Opera House." *The Bee*. Washington, D. C. May 3, 1884.

"Fort Fisher, Second Battle of Fort Fisher." https://www.civilwar.org/learn/civil-war/battles/fort-fisher Accessed March 20, 2018.

"Fort Fisher State Historic Site." http://www.nchistoricsites.org/fisher/ Accessed March 16, 2018."

The Freeman. Indianapolis, IN. December 7, 1889.

Freeman, Elise; Wynell Burroughs Schamel, and Jean West. "The Fight for Equal Rights: A Recruiting Poster for Black Soldiers in the Civil War." *Social Education* 56, 2 (February 1992. 118-120.

"Gardiner, James." http://www.homeofheroes.com/moh/citations_1862_cwa/gardiner_james.html Accessed April 6, 2018.

"Gardiner, James." https://www.nps.gov/rich/learn/historyculture/gardiner.htm Accessed April 6, 2018.

Gerth, Adrian. "The Gibraltar of the South." https://capefearlivingmagazine.com/the-gibraltar-of-the-south Accessed March 20, 2018.

Gilkes, Paul. "Joachim Pease Medal of Honor from Civil War on public display in Washington, D.C." https://www.coinworld.com/news/us-coins/2017/10/joachim-pease-congressional-medal-of-honor.all.htm Accessed April 13, 2018.

Gorman, Ron. "The Battle of New Market Heights: the 5th USCT's 'Glory.' http://www.Oberlinheritagecenter.org/blog/2014/09/the-battle-of-new-market-heights-the-5th-uscts-glory/ Accessed March 21, 2018.

Gragg, Rod. *Confederate Goliath: The Battle of Fort Fisher*. Baton Rouge: Louisiana State University.

The Greater Atlanta Buffalo Soldiers. "William H. Brown-Medal of Honor." https:www.facebook.com/permalink/php?id=1533332710226719&story_fbid=1692271397666182 Accessed April 5, 2018.

"Ground Breaking for U.S. Colored Troop Memorial Monument, March 4, 2012, in Lexington Park, Maryland." https://jubiloemancipationcentry.wordpress.com/tag/sgt-james-h-harris/ Accessed April 6, 2018.

Hamilton, Lowell D. "The Battle of Honey Hill, South Carolina." Nd.

Hammond, Thomas M. "William H. Carney: 54th Massachusetts Soldier and First Black U. S. Medal of Honor Recipient." *America's Civil War*. January 29, 2007 n.p.

Hanna, Charles W. *African American recipients of the Medal of Honor: a biographical dictionary, Civil War through Vietnam War*. McFarland and Company, Inc., 2010.

Harris, Hamil R., Smith, Leef. "On Memorial Day, Soldiers and Citizens Honor Sacrifices of Those Who Fought for Freedom." *The Washington Post*. May 27, 1997. p. B12.

"Harris, James H." https://www.nps.gov/rich/learn/historyculture/harris.htm Accessed April 6, 2018.

Hartwell, Alfred. "Personal Reminiscences of the Civil War. Paper Read Before Honolulu Social Club. 1903.

Hedelt, Rob. "Upcoming Stratford Hall program to detail heroics of medal-winning African American sailor." *The Free Lance-Star*. February 8, 2018.

Heinatz, Stephanie. "Born a Slave, Bred a Soldier." http://www.dailypress.com/news/black-history/dp-7654sy0jul26-story.html Accessed April 13, 2018.

-----. "Changing Times and Failing Body." http://www.dailypress.com/news/black-history/dp-79099sy0jul29-story.html Accessed April 13, 2018.

-----. "Cheesecake Cemetery." http://www.dailypress.com/news/black-history/dp-71927sy0jul24-story.html Accessed April 13, 2018.

-----. "Living With Ghosts." http://ww.dailypress.com/news/black-history/dp-medalj123jul23-story.html Accessed April 13, 2018.

-----. "A man's milestone." http://www.dailypress.com/news/black-history/dp-93354sy0aug06-story.html Accessed April 16, 2018.

-----. "A Saga Set in Stone." http://www.dailypress.com/news/black-history/dp-77642sy0jul30-story.html Accessed April 16, 2018.

-----. "Visiting Cheesecake Cemetery." https://www.dailypress.com/news/black-history/dp-77503sy0jul28-story.html Accessed April 16, 2018.

-----. "With Great Gallantry." https://www.dailypress.com/news/black-history/dp-civilwar5jul26-story.html Accessed April 16, 2018.

Helm, Matt. "Carney, William H." www.blackpast.org/aah/carney-william-h-1840-1908 Accessed April 5, 2018.

"Heroes of Camden, New Jersey: Landsman John Lawson." http://www.dvrbs.com/CW/CamdenCountyHeroes-JohnLawson.htm Accessed April 12, 2018.

"Hilton, Alfred B." https://www.nps.gov/rich/learn/historyculture/hilton.htm Accessed April 6, 2018.

Hirtle, John. "The Seacoast's Civil War Star." *Atlantic News Beach Guide, 2004*. Hampton, NH.

"Historical Marker Honors Former Slave Who Raised Civil War Regiment." https://www.ohio-forum.com/2013/11/historical-marker-honors-former-slave-who-raised-civil-war-regiment Accessed April 10, 2018.

"History of Mr. Lawson." Program from April 24, 2004 ceremony for John H. Lawson at Mt. Peace Cemetery in Lawnside, NJ.

"History of the Colored Troops in the American Civil War." https://americancivilwar.com/colored/histofcoloredtroops.html Accessed April 19, 2018.

"Holland Letter 1." http://www.nps.gov/rich/learn/historyculture.mhletter1.htm Accessed April 10, 2018.

"Holland, Milton M." https://www.nps.gov/rich/learn/historyculture/holland.htm Accessed April 10, 2018.

https://gozips.com/sports/2017/5/25/athletics-facilities-rifle.aspx Accessed July 17, 2019.

https://www.nps.gov/pete/learn/historyculture/the-crater.htm Accessed January 5, 2019.

https://themedalofhonor.com/medal-of-honor-recipients/recipients/smith-andrew-civil-war; www.cmohs.org---smith, a j Accessed April 13, 2018.

Hyman, Carolyn. "Holland, Spearman." *Handbook of Texas Online*. http:/www/tshonline.org/ handbook/online/articles/fho28 Accessed April 10, 2018.

"Iowa Civil War Monuments." http://www.iowacivilwarmonuments.com/cgi-bin/gaard-details.pl?1227230506-2 Accessed April 18, 2018.

"James Daniel Gardner." https://www.findagrave.com/memorial/7661519/james-daniel-gardner Accessed April 6, 2018.

"James H. Bronson." https://valormilitarytimes.com Accessed April 3, 2018.

"James H. Harris." http://www.arlingtoncemetery.net/jhharris.htm Accessed April 6, 2018.

"James Mifflin." https://www.findagrave.com/memorial/11704845/james-mifflin Accessed April 12, 2018.

"James Mifflin." https://www.peoplemaven.com/p/rG613w/james-mifflin Accessed April 12, 2018.

"James, Miles." https://www.nps.gov/rich/learn/historyculture/james.htm Accessed April 18, 2018.

Jenkins, Mark F. "MOH: Landsman John Lawson." https://civilwartalk.com/threads/moh-landsman-john-lawson.115657 Accessed April 12, 2018.

"Joachim Pease." https://howlingpixel.com/i-en/Joachim_Pease Accessed July 8, 2019.

"Joachim Pease." https://www.findagrave.com/memorial/12791169/joachim-pease Accessed April 13, 2018.

"John Henry Lawson." https://www.findagrave.com/memorial/7197017/john-henry-lawson Accessed April 12, 2018.

"John H. Lawson, Medal of Honor Recipient." http://americanhistory.si.edu/collections/search/object/nmah_1438234 Accessed April 12, 2018.

"John Lawson." http://snowhillgenealogy.com/SecondSite/CWBLv8_1116113-o/p74.htm Accessed April 12, 2018.

"John Lawson: Sailor Aboard the U.S.S. Hartford." https://ncnwjax.wordpress.com/2015/02/03/john-lawson-1837-1919-sailor-aboard-the-u-s-s-hartford Accessed April 12, 2018.

Johnson, Yvonne. "MD22 bridge memorializes Civil War Soldier, Harco Medal of Honor recipient." APG NEWS. November 16, 2017.

Jones, Jae. "Alexander Kelly: Awarded the Medal of Honor for Actions at the Battle of Chaffin's Farm in Virginia." https://blackthen.com/alexander-kelly-awarded-medal-honor-actions-battle-chaffins-farm-virginia Accessed April 10, 2018.

-----."Powhatan Beaty: Actor & Soldier Decorated with United States Medal of Honor."n.d.

----. "Robert Blake: Union Navy Sailor During the American Civil War." January 23, 2018. https://blackthen.com/robert-blake-union-navy-sailor-american-civil-war Accessed March 21, 2018.

"June 19—Happy Birthday Bruce Anderson." The Amsterdam, NY Blog Accessed March 20, 2018.

Kammen, Carol. "Guest Essay: Black Troops, White Civil War Units" http://newyorkhistoryblog.org/2012/01/23/guest-essay-black-troops-white-civil-war-units/ Accessed March 20, 2018.

Katz, William Loren. "Six New Medal of Honor Men: William H. Brown, Wilson Brown, William Loren Katz, Adam Paine." *Journal of Negro History*. January 1968. 70-80.

kentuckyguard. "Corporal Andrew Jackson Smith, Kentucky's only African-American Civil War Medal of Honor recipient." http://kentuckyguard.dodlive.mil/2015/02/09/corporal-andrew-jackson-smith-kentuckys-only-african-american-civil-war-medal-of-honor-recipient Accessed April 13, 2018.

Kienle, Polly. "Black Men in Navy Blue: John H. Lawson and William B. Gould." https://www.nps.gov/articles/lawson-and-gould.htm Accessed April 12, 2018.

Kimberlin, Joanne. "In Chesapeake, black soldiers' legacy not forgotten." https://pilotonline.com/news/article_cd4a231f-65f7-54db-b723-e101687d3597.html Accessed April 18, 2018.

Landsman, Danie. "The Fall of Fort Fisher." https://www.civilwar.org/learn/articles/fall-fort-fisher Accessed March 20, 2018.

Lange, Katie. "Meet Sgt. William Carney: The First African American Medal of Honor Recipient." DoD News, Defense Media Activity. n.p. n.d.
Langston, John Mercer. *From the Virginia Plantation to the National Capitol.* Hartford, CT. 1894.
"Lawnside Resident Pays Ultimate Respect To Hero." *Camden Courier Courier-Post.* February 22, 2004.
Leatherwood, Art. "Whiting, William Henry Chase." https://tshaonline.org/handbook/online/articles/fwhew Accessed July 8, 2018.
Lewis, David. "Fleetwood, Christian Abraham." http://www.blackpast.org/aah/fleetwood-christian-abraham-1840-1914 Accessed April 6, 2018.
Lucko, Paul M. "Holland, Milton M." https://tshonline.org/handbook/online/articles.fhobt Accessed April 10, 2018.
Mainstd. "Unsung authors at the Historical Society of Harford County." http://www.belairartsandentertainment.org/2014/01/14/2545 Accessed April 18, 2018.
Mangus, Mike. "5th Regiment United States Colored Troops (1861-1865)." August 6, 2011. Ohio State University.
Marcois, Bart. "Powhatan Beaty: Hero, Engineer, Actor, Playwright, Father." https://www.Opslens.com/2018/02/02/powhatan-beaty-hero-black-history-month/ Accessed March 21, 2018.
Margolis, Cyrene. "Robert A. Pinn: Distinguished service in war and peace." http://www.cantonrep.com/article/20120430/News/304309861 Accessed April 17, 2018.
"Maryland Society to Display Rare USCT Flag." Baltimore Civil War Roundtable. Nd.
"Mattox Creek." https://www.revolvy.com/main/index.php?s=Mattox+Creek&item_type=topic Accessed March 20, 2018.
McIlvain, Myra H. "Former Texas Slaves Serve in Civil War." https://myrahmcilvain.com/2013/12/20/former-texas-slaves-serve-in-civil-war Accessed April 10, 2018.
McRae, Bennie. "Resting Place of Landsman Wilson Brown and hundreds Union Army/NavyCivil War soldiers and sailors." lestweforget.hamptonu.edu/page.cfm?uuid=9FEC3293-E6EC-61F1-958D30F235422C4F Accessed April 5, 2018.
----. "Union Navy: Wilson Brown and Tom Gates." www.afrigeneas.com/forum-militaryarchive/archive/index.cgi/md/read/id/720/sbj/union-navy-wilson-brown-and-tom-gates Accessed April 5, 2018.
"Meade to Dahlgren," *ORN*, 15:190-191.
"Medal of Honor: Christian A. Fleetwood." http://www.civilwar.si.edu/soldiering_medal_of_honor.html Accessed April 6, 2018.
"Medal of Honor: Heroes of the Battle of Chaffin's Farm." https://www.cem.va.gov/CEM/pdf/Medal_of_Honor_Narratives_Heroes_Chapins_Farm.pdf Accessed July 8, 2018.

"Medal of Honor Recipients—Civil War (A-L)." http://www.history.army.mil/html/moh/civwaral.html Accessed April 5, 2018.

----- (M-Z." http://www.history.army.mil/html/moh/civwarmz.html Accessed April 5, 2018.

"Medal of Honor Winners on the American Civil War Memorial." http://www.isisinform.com/medal-of-honor-winners-on-the-african-american-civil-war-memorial/ Accessed April 12, 2018.

The Messenger. Athens, Ohio. February 4, 1864.

"Miles James." https://billiongraves.com/grave/Miles-James/14524162 Accessed April 18, 2018.

"Miles James enlisted." https://www.facebook.com/TheHstryMakers/posts/1326194834094895 Accessed April 10, 2018.

Miles, Suzannah Smith. "Legareville once a happy, summer village." https://www.moultrienews.com/archives/legareville-once-a-happy-summer-village/article_be3a11d6-655a-5cb7acd7-507702e8402f.html Accessed April 2, 2018.

"Milton Holland, born August 1st, 1844." http://civilwaref.blogspot.com/2013/08/milton-holland-born-august-1st-1844.html Accessed April 10, 2018.

"Milton M. Holland." http://www.cemetery.state.tx.us/pub/user_form.asp?pers_id=11147 Accessed April 10, 2018.

"Milton M. Holland, a Civil War soldier, was the first Texan to be awarded the Medal of Honor." http://hollandhistory.blogspot.com/2014/09/milton-m-holland-civil-war-soldier-was.html Accessed April 10, 2018.

"Milton M. Holland: Sergeant Major, United States Army." http://www.arlingtoncemetery.net/mholland.htm Accessed April 10, 2018.

Moss, Juanita Patience. *The Forgotten Black Soldiers in White Regiments During the Civil War.* Westminster, Maryland: Heritage Books. 2008.

Mumper, Wes. "Col. David L. Stricker Camp #64 SUVCW Delaware." https://www.facebook.com/strickersuvcw/posts/726225370778418 Accessed April 6, 2018.

Murray, Shannon D. "Civil War novelist conveys 'real story' of black soldiers through life of local hero." *Baltimore Sun.* July 17, 1994.

"National Guard Militia Museum of New Jersey." https://www.facebook.com/127004387321616/photos/pb.127004387321616.-2207520000.1469301694./1131412973547414/?type=3 Accessed April 6, 2018.

"Navy Medals Rescinded." http://www.homeofheroes.com/moh/corrections/purge_navy.html Accessed April 6, 2018.

Nichols, Ben. "James H. Bronson." http://ranger95.com/civil_war_us/us_color_troops/infantry/5usct/james_h_bronson_d_5usct.htm Accessed April 4, 2018.

Official Records of the Union and Confederate navies in the War of the Rebellion. Washington, D.C.: Government Printing Office, 1897.

"Ohio National Guard Photo Gallery." https://ong.ohio.gov/images/photo-galleries/2015-02.html Accessed July 18, 2019.

"On the Battlefield." https://www.nps.gov/parkhistory/online_books/civil_war_series/2/sec18.htm Accessed April 4, 2018.

"127th Regiment Ohio Volunteer Infantry." https://ww.ohiocivilwarcentral.com/entry.php?rec=790 Accessed April 13, 2018.

Opinde, Walter. "A Brave Black Man at the Warfront: Sergeant William Carney Harvey. [sic]" https: blackthen.com/brave-man-warfront-sergeant-william-carney-harvey Accessed April 5, 2018.

Patrick, Bethanne Kelly. "Sgt. William H. Carney." https://www.military.com/history/sgt-william-h-carney.html Accessed April 5, 2018.

Patterson, Michael Robert. "William H. Brown." http://www.arlingtoncemetery.net/whbrown.htm Accessed April 5, 2018.

Percoco, Jim. "The United States Colored Troops." https://civilwar.org/learn/articles/united-states-colored-troops Accessed March 20, 2018.

Perdreau, Connie. "A Biographical Sketch of Master Sergeant Milton Holland." http:grosvenor-cwrt.org/our-moh-recipients/more-about-master-sergeant-milton-holland Accessed April 10, 2018.

Phisterer, Frederick. *New York in the War of the Rebellion.* Albany: J. B. Lyon Company. 1912.

"Photo of Grave site of MOH Recipient Bruce Anderson." http://www.homeofheroes.com/gravesites/states/pages_af/Anderson.bruce_ny.html Accessed March 16, 2018.

Piggott, Mark O. "Civil War Hero Remembered at Yorktown Black History Month Celebration." *Navy News Service.* February 25, 2011.

"Pinn, Robert." https://www.nps.gov/rich/learn/historyculture/pinn.htm. Accessed April 13, 2018.

"Pinn, Robert Alexander." http://www.blackpast.org/aah/pinn-robert-alexander-1843-1911 Accessed April 19, 2018.

"Pinn's left hand." www.loc.gov/podcasts/african-american-passages/episode3.html Accessed July 20, 2019.

Pohanka, Brian C. "Fort Wagner and the 54th Massachusetts Volunteer Infantry." https://www.civilwar.org/learn/articles/fort-wagner-and-54th-massachusetts-volunteer-infantry Accessed March 20, 2018.

"Powhatan Beaty, born October 8, 1837." http://civilwaref/blogspot.com/2013/10/powhatan-beaty-born-october-8-1837.html Accessed March 21, 2018.

"Powhatan Beaty is Dead." *The Labor Advocate.* Cincinnati, Ohio. December 6, 1916.

Price, Jimmy. "Profile in Courage: Sergeant-Major Thomas R. Hawkins, 6th USCT." http://sablearm.blogspot.com/2010/06/profile-in-courage-sergeant-major.html Accessed April 6, 2018.

----- "Profile in Courage: Sgt. James Gardner, Co. I 36th USCT." http://sablearm.blogspot.com/2010/08/profile-in-courage-sgt-james-gardner-co.html Accessed April 6, 2018.

"PVT Bruce Anderson." https://www.findagrave.com/memorial/5747861/bruce-anderson Accessed March 16, 2018.

"PVT Charles Veale." https://www.findagrave.com/memorial/7895208/charles-veale Accessed April 18, 2018.

Ralston, Gary. "Sgt. William H. Barnes—MOH." http://indianolatx.com/BarnesWH.html Accessed March 16, 2018.

"Ratcliff, Edward." https://www.nps.gov/rich/learn/historyculture/ratcliff.htm Accessed April 13, 2018.

Ratcliffe, Robert. "The Sons of Bird Holland." http://ratcliffe.com/SonsofBirdHolland/category/bird-holland. Accessed April 10, 2018.

Reagen, James E. "African Americans fought at Fort Fisher." *The Daily News*. February 11, 2016. http://www.thedailynewsonline.com/blogs/african-americans-fought-at-fort-Fisher-20160211 Accessed March 16, 2018.

-----. "Our Forgotten Heroes of Fort Fisher." *The Daily News*. February 18, 2016. http://www.ogd.com/blogs/our-forgotten-heroes-of-fort-fisher-20160218 Accessed March 16, 2018.

Regan, Christopher J. "The American flag, Medal of Honor and the President." http://www.montgomery-herald-com/opinion/the-american-flag-medal-of-honor-and-the-president/article_d74af260-a8bc-11e7-9701-93647d713c50html Accessed April 16, 2018.

Regimental History: 38th U. S. Colored Troops. http://civilwarintheeast.com/USA/US/USCT38.php Accessed March 16, 2018.

"Return of a Death in the City of Philadelphia—1886," no. 1139. Philadelphia Municipal Archives.

"Rhumb Lines." Navy Office of Information. January 14, 2009.

"Richmond National Battlefield Park and Medal of Honor Monument." http://www.aahistoric-sitesva.org/items/show/360?tour=3&index=6 Accessed April 6, 2018

"Robert Blake: Slave, Contraband, Sailor, and Hero." https://markerhunter.wordpress.com/2013/12/26/robert-blake Accessed March 21, 2018.

"Robert Pinn." https://www.hmdb.org/marker.asp?marker=61478 Accessed April 13, 2018.

Rozen-Wheeler, Adam. "Smith, Andrew Jackson." http://www.blackpast.org/aah/smith-andrew-jackson-1843-1932 Accessed April 13, 2018.

Sagely, Pamela. "Two Indiana County veterans to be inducted into Hall of Valor." http://triblive.com/news/Indiana/5747360-74/prola-valor.hall Accessed April 4, 2018.

"Sanderson, Aaron." http://www.homeofhearoes.com/moh/citations_1862_cwq/sanderson.html Accessed March 20, 2018.

Sandoval, Timothy. "Church holds presentation on African-American contributions to the Civil War." *Carroll County Times.* Westminster, Maryland. February 24, 2014.

Schemmer, Clint. "Black soldiers 'silenced every cavil of the doubters.'" http://www.Fredericksburg.com/features/black-soldiers-silenced-every-cavil-of-the-doubters/article_f31f9c29-3e16-59e3-ad39-e7e90af6f9b8.html Accessed March 21, 2018.

Scott, Donald. "Alexander Kelly" http://pacivilwar150.com/ThroughPeople/AfricanAmericans/AlexanderKelly.html Accessed April 10, 2018.

"7 Historical Civil War Figures Who Don't Have a Statue, But Deserve One." HuffPost Partner Studio. January 11, 2017.

"SGT Alfred B. Hilton." https://www.findagrave.com/memorial/7895145/alfred.b.hilton Accessed April 6, 2018.

"Sgt. Alfred B. Hilton Bridge dedication set for Thursday, Nov. 9." http://www.baltimoresun.com/news/maryland/harford/aegis/ph-ag-hilton-bridge-dedication-preview-20171107-story.html Accessed April 6, 2018.

"SGT Andrew Jackson Smith." https:www.findagrave.com/memorial/8762808/andrew-jackson-smith Accessed April 13. 2018.

"Sgt Maj Thomas R. Hawkins." https://www.findagrave.com/memorial/7101904/thomas-r.-hawkins Accessed April 6, 2018.

"Sgt. William Carney, Jr. (1840-1908) Medal of Honor Recipient." https://americacomesalive.com/2013/05/28/sgt-william-carney-jr-1840-1908-medal-of-honor-recipient Accessed April 5, 2018.

"SGT James H. Harris." https://www.findagrave.com/memorial/18822/james-h.-harris Accessed April 6, 2018.

"SGT William Harvey Carney." https://findagrave.com/memorial/6826582/william-harvey-carney Accessed April 5, 2018.

Sicher, Peter A. "The African American Heroes of New Market Heights." https://www.civilwar.org/learn/articles/covered-glory Accessed April 3, 2018.

"6th Regiment U. S. Colored Troop, Company F." http://www.pa-roots.com/pacw/usct/6thusc/6thusctcof.html Accessed April 18, 2018.

"The Sloop of War, Kearsarge." http://www.warner.nh.us/ships.htm Accessed April 13, 2018.

"Smith, Andrew Jackson." http://www.cmohs.org/recipient-detail/1261/smith-andrew-jackson.php Accessed April 13, 2018.

Smith, Carletta. "June 19, 1864: The Battle of Cherbourg Occurs." https://blackthen.com/june-19, 1864-battle-cherbourg-occurs/ Accessed April 19, 2018.

Sparks, Cheryl M. "MDTA Dedicates MD 22 Bridge over I-95 to Harford County Civil War Veteran." http://www.mdot.maryland.gov/News/Releases2017/2017_Nov_9_Bridge_Dedicated_to_Civil_War_Hero." Accessed April 18, 2018.

"Stark's Famous: Robert Pinn." http://www.inde-online.com/news/20161021/starks-famous-robert-pinn Accessed April 13, 2018.

Steelman, Ben. "Black soldier persevered for Medal of Honor." Star News Online. http://www.stamewsonline.com/news/20150228/black-soldier-persevered-for-medal-of-honor Accessed March 16, 2018.

Stern, Nicholas C. "Local family commemorates Civil War hero." *Frederick News-Post*. Frederick, Maryland. August 17, 2008.

Stewart, Selma. "USCT James Daniel Gardner Honored." *Daily Press*, Newport News, VA. May 25, 2006.

"Stories." https://www.nps.gov/afam/learn/historyculture/stories.htm Accessed April 19, 2018.

Sturgill, Erika Quesenbery. "Alfred Hilton: Harford's Medal of Honor recipient." http://www.cecildaily.com/barganeer/alfred-hilton-harford-s-medal-of-honor-recipient/article_c46d73b8-b469-5d7d-8b4e-6b03e16c7acc.html Accessed April 6, 2018.

Talbot, Tim. "Corporal Miles James-A Superior Soldier." http://randomthoughtsonhistory.blogspot.com/2017/10/corporal-miles-james-superior-soldier.html Accessed April 10, 2018.

-----. "Fort Wright: The Black Brigade." http://explorekyhistory.ky.gov/items/show/96?tour=9&index=21 Accessed March 21, 2018.

-----. "Personality Spotlight: Christian Fleetwood." http://randomthoughtsonhistory.blogspot.com/2017/11/personality-spotlight-christian.html Accessed April 6, 2018.

"38th Regiment, United States Colored Infantry." https://web.archive.org/web/20080410173040/www.itd.nps.gov/cwss/regiments.cfm Accessed March 16, 2018.

"38th United States Colored Troops." http://civilwarintheeast.com/us-regiments-batteries/us-Colored-troops/38th-united-states-colored-troops Accessed April 17, 2018.

"36th U.S. Colored Infantry Medal of Honor Winners." http://www.ncgenweb.us/ncusct/medals.htm Accessed April 6, 2018.

"Thomas R. Hawkins." https://www.hmdb.org/marker.asp?marker=74789 Accessed April 18, 2018.

"Thomas R. Hawkins." http://philadelphiaencyclopedia.org/3c18559r-2 Accessed April 6, 2018.

"Three Medals of Honor—by Don Troiani." http://www.framingfox.com/tmeofhobycoh.html Accessed April 18, 2018.

"Today in Black History, 12/6/2011." http://thewright.org/explore/exhibitions/581-witness-the-art-of-jerry-pinkney Accessed March 21, 2018.

"Today in Black History, 7/11/2012." https://www.thewright.org/index.php/explore/educational-resources/2013-11-28-11-27-37/today-in-black-history-7112012 Accessed April 6, 2012.

"Today in Black History, 7/27/2014." https://thewright.org/index.php/explore/educational-resources/2013-11-28-11-27-37/today-in-black-history-7272014 Accessed April 16, 2018.

Todd, Tom. "SGT William H Barnes." https://www.findagrave.com/memorial/18172/william-h-barnes Accessed March 16, 2018.

The Union army: a history of military affairs in the loyal states, 1861-65—records of the regiments in the Union army—cyclopedia of battles---memoirs of commanders and soldiers. Vol. II. Madison, WI. Federal Publishing Company. 1908.

"United States Colored Troops: Civil War Memorial Monument." https://www.hmdb.org/marker.asp?marker=56476 Accessed March 20, 2018.

"United States Colored Troops: 4th Regiment Infantry." https://www.nps.gov/rich/learn/historyculture/4thusct.htm Accessed April 16, 2018.

"United States Colored Troops: 39th Regiment, United States Colored Infantry." https://www.nps.gov/civilwar/search-battle-units-detail.htm?battleUnitCode=UUS0039RI00C Accessed April 17, 2018.

"United States Colored Troops: 36th Regiment Infantry." https://www.nps.gov/rich/learn/historyculture/36thusct.htm Accessed April 18, 2018.

"United States Colored Troops (USCT) Civil War Memorial Monument." https://www.ucaconline.org/historic-monuments-and-statues.html Accessed April 18, 2018.

"*U.S.S. Brooklyn.*" http://www.navsourc.org/archives/09/86/86052.htm Accessed April 12, 2018.

"*USS Hartford*: *Civil War-Era Warship, Sinks at its Berth in Norfolk VA Navy Yard.*" http: www.burnpit.us/2014/11/uss-hartford-civil-war-era-warship-sinks-its-berth-norfolk-va-navy-yard Accessed April 19, 2018.

"*USS Marblehead.*" http://www.navsource.org/archives/09/86/86330.htm Accessed April 2, 2018.

"*USS Mifflin.*" https://www.navsource.org/archives/10/01/03207.htm Accessed April 12, 2018.

Vasquez, Ryan. "150th Anniversary of the Battle of Mobile Bay." n.d.

"Veal Charles." https://www.nps.gov/rich/learn/historyculture/veal.htm Accessed April 16, 2018

Virginia Foundation for the Humanities. "Richmond National Battlefield Park and Medal of Honor Monument." http://www.aahistoricsitesva.org/items/show/360?tour=3&index=6 Accessed April 3, 2018.

Vought, Allan. "Alfred Hilton, Harford's only Medal of Honor recipient." http://www.baltimoresun.com.news/maryland/harford/aegis/retro-alfred-hilton-20161104-story.html Accessed April 6, 2018.

Walker, Richard. "Ex-slave, Medal of Honor recipient, remembered with naming of DMV."

http://theandd.com/news/local/ex-slave-medal-of-honor-recipient-remembered-with-naming-of/article_cc2bea50-519b-11e3-a886-001a4bcf887a.html Accessed April 2, 2018.

Wertz, Frederick. "For love of Old Glory: Civil War Medals of Honor." https://blog.findmy-past.com/community/frederick_wertz Accessed April 16, 2018.

"West Gulf Blockading Squadron." https://www.nps.gov/wicr/learn/historyculture/brown-navy.htm Accessed April 17, 2018.

Whitacre, Paula Tarnapol. "Sgt. Major Christian Fleetwood: USCT Member, Medal of Honor Recipient, Diary Keeper. http://www.paulawhitacre.com/blog/2017/9/13/christian.fleetwood Accessed April 6, 2018.

"Who was the first black person to win the congressional Medal of Honor?" https://socratic.org/questions/who-was-the-first-black-person-to-win-the-congressional-medal-of-honor Accessed April 3, 2018.

"Who Were These Heroes?" *Negro History Bulletin*. Vol. 23, No. 3, December 1959. Pp. 50, 69-70.

"William H. Barnes." http://msa.maryland.gov/megafile/msa/speccol/sc3500/sc3520/004600/004684/html/04684bio.html Accessed March 16, 2018.

William H. Barnes---Compiled service record from http://www.calhouncountyhc.org/Marker_BarnesWH.pdf Accessed March 16, 2018.

"William H. Brown." https://findagrave.com/memorial/18821/william-h.-brown Accessed April 5, 2018.

"William H. Carney at Fort Wagner." Housedivided.dickinson.edu/grandreview/2010/06/04/william-h-carney-at-fort-wagner Accessed April 5, 2018.

"William H. Carney: First Black American to merit the Medal of Honor." Kentakepage.com/william-h-carney-first-black-american-to-merit-the-medal-of-honor. Accessed April 5, 2018.

"Wilson Brown." http://www.homeofheroes.com/gravesites/states/pages_af/brown_wilson_ms.html Accessed April 5, 2018.

"Wilson Brown: Medal of Honor recipient." http://enacademic.com/dic.nsf/enwiki/4688343 Accessed April 5, 2018.

Wise, Stephen R. "Honey Hill, Battle of." http://www.scencyclopedia.org/sce/entries/honey-hill-battle-of Accessed April 13, 2018.

Wordbone. "Tales of Two Cities." http://writing-the-wrongs.blogspot.com/2011/05/decatur-dorsey.html Accessed April 6, 2018.

The Wright Blogger. "Today in Black History: 1/24/2014." https://thewright.org/index.php/explore/educational-resources/2013-11-27-37/today-in-black-history-1242014 Accessed April 5, 2018.

www.peachamhistorical.org/wp-content/uploads/2016/06/PHA_Patriot_Summer_2011.pdf Accessed December 31, 2018.

www.racetimeplace.com/medalofhonor.htm Accessed December 31, 2018.

"*Wyandank*." http://www.navsource.org/archives/09/86/86063.htm Accessed March 16, 2018.

ABOUT THE AUTHOR

A retired Tennessee teacher, Randy Bishop now teaches for the North Tippah School District in Mississippi and serves as an adjunct history professor for Jackson State Community College. He is president of the local library board and a city councilman in his hometown. Bishop is a member of several historical associations and preservation groups and has previously published articles as well as ten books, including The Tennessee Brigade, Tennessee's Civil War Battlefields, Mississippi's Civil War Battlefields, Kentucky's Civil War Battlefields, Civil War Generals of Tennessee, A Civil War Devotional, Mississippi's Civil War Generals, Sacrifices of the Porters, and The Trail, and Marching for Union. Randy and his wife Sharon, also a teacher, reside in Middleton, Tennessee and are the parents of two grown sons, Jay and Ben.

www.ingramcontent.com/pod-product-compliance
Lightning Source LLC
LaVergne TN
LVHW091543060526
838200LV00036B/687